WOMEN WRITING RESISTANCE

D0885763

WOMEN WRITING RESISTANCE

ESSAYS ON
LATIN AMERICA
AND THE CARIBBEAN

Edited by
Jennifer Browdy

BEACON PRESS · BOSTON

Beacon Press
Boston, Massachusetts
www.beacon.org

Beacon Press books
are published under the auspices of
the Unitarian Universalist Association of Congregations.

20 19 18 17   8 7 6 5 4 3 2 1

This book is printed on acid-free paper that meets the uncoated paper
ANSI/NISO specifications for permanence as revised in 1992.

Text design and composition by Kim Arney

Gloria Anzaldúa, "Speaking in Tongues: A Letter to Third World Women Writers."
From *This Bridge Called My Back*, ed. by Gloria Anzaldúa and Cherríe Moraga.
San Francisco: Kitchen Table/Women of Color Press, 1983;
© Gloria E. Anzaldúa Literary Trust.

Excerpt from *A Small Place* by Jamaica Kincaid. Copyright © 1988 by Jamaica Kincaid.
Reprinted by permission of Farrar, Straus, and Giroux, LLC.

Rigoberta Menchú, "The Quincentenary Conference and the Earth Summit, 1992."
From *Crossing Borders*, trans. by Anne Wright. London: Verso, 1998;
reprinted with permission from Verso.

Judith Ortiz Cofer, "The Myth of the Latin Woman." From *The Latin Deli:
Telling the Lives of Barrio Women*. New York: W. W. Norton, 1993;
reprinted with permission from the University of Georgia Press.

Library of Congress Cataloging-in-Publication Data
Names: Browdy, Jennifer, editor.
Title: Women writing resistance : essays on Latin America and the Caribbean /
edited by Jennifer Browdy.
Description: Boston, Massachusetts : Beacon Press, [2017] | Includes bibliographical references.
Identifiers: LCCN 2017005850 | ISBN 9780807088197 (pbk. : alk. paper) |
ISBN 9780807088203 (e-book)
Subjects: LCSH: Social justice—Latin America. | Social justice—Caribbean Area. | Latin
America—Social conditions. | Caribbean Area—Social conditions. | Ethnicity—Caribbean
Area. | Ethnicity—Latin America. | Women—Latin America—Social conditions. | Women—
Caribbean Area—Social conditions.
Classification: LCC HN110.5.A8 W66 2017 | DDC 303.3/72098—dc23
LC record available at https://lccn.loc.gov/2017005850

CONTENTS

Preface to the 2003 Edition   vii
Elizabeth Martinez

Introduction   1
Jennifer Browdy

PART ONE: RE-ENVISIONING HISTORY

1 Revision   15
Aurora Levins Morales

2 We Are Ugly, but We Are Here   21
Edwidge Danticat

3 The Silent Witness   27
Raquel Partnoy

4 And What Would It Be Like?   39
Michelle Cliff

5 Everything I Kept: Reflections of an "Anthropoeta"   45
Ruth Behar

6 The Dream of *Nunca Más*: Healing the Wounds   59
Emma Sepúlveda

PART TWO: THE POLITICS OF LANGUAGE AND IDENTITY

7 Speaking in Tongues: A Letter to Third World Women Writers   69
Gloria Anzaldúa

8 Las aeious   82
Ruth Irupé Sanabria

9 Art in América con Acento   92
Cherríe Moraga

10 The Myth of the Latin Woman   101
   Judith Ortiz Cofer

11 The Quincentenary Conference and the Earth Summit, 1992 109
   Rigoberta Menchú

PART THREE: STRATEGIES OF RESISTANCE

12 A Small Place   133
   Jamaica Kincaid

13 One Precious Moment   144
   Margaret Randall

14 On Being Shorter: How Our Testimonial Texts
   Defy the Academy   161
   Alicia Partnoy

15 Death in the Desert: The Women of Ciudad Juárez   184
   Marjorie Agosín

16 I Came to Help: Resistance Writ Small   203
   Julia Alvarez

   Afterword: *No Pare, Sigue Sigue:* Refilling the Resistance Well 205
   Veronica Chambers

   Acknowledgments   208
   Contributor Biographies   210
   Selected Bibliography   218

PREFACE TO THE 2003 EDITION

– Elizabeth Martinez –

"THIS EXTRAORDINARY COLLECTION . . ." I could begin that way, but no. Those words, though true enough, seem all too inadequate. The book is—here comes a risky claim—revolutionary. But why? An encouraging number of anthologies of writings by women of color have appeared in recent years, with *This Bridge Called My Back*, edited by Gloria Anzaldúa and Cherríe Moraga, leading the way. That development ended decades of invisibility. Now comes Jennifer Browdy's book, offering new reasons to celebrate.

There is, first, the welcome fact that her book focuses on Latin America and the Caribbean, those huge expanses of our hemisphere too often ignored or minimized in the past. Except for academic specialists, few people, even on the left, paid much attention to Latin America until thousands of indigenous rebels rose up in southern Mexico [in 1994, in response to the North American Free Trade Agreement]. And the Caribbean exists in the minds of many North Americans mostly thanks to a unique, struggling revolution in Cuba that won't go away. Although we see more attention given to this region today, there is still too little awareness of the many peoples, histories, and cultures that the women writers in this book so eloquently and passionately illuminate.

Their stories of resistance to oppression are also global, for the conditions they present exist worldwide. These writers cry out against the effects of colonization, unfettered imperialism, and corporate globalization on billions of people, as well as on the planet itself. Their rage is haunting. Who can forget the saying of poor Haitian women under slavery and colonial oppression, as recalled here by Edwidge Danticat: "We are ugly, but we are here"? And here to stay, Danticat adds. "Every once in a while, we must scream this as far as the wind can carry our voices," she writes.

The book's call for such defiance is not new. Since September 11, 2001, the need for it has been greater than ever, as the US response to that dreadful day continues sending its dreadful message: ours is an age of intensified empire-building in which no war is unthinkable.

It is also an age of galloping globalization for the benefit of capitalist growth. In our hemisphere, the suffering caused by NAFTA has not halted the drive toward more of the same alphabet. Today's "Free Trade Area of the Americas" (FTAA), and a similar plan for Central America (CAFTA), move forward that caravan of misery.

Around the world we find institutions like the World Trade Organization (WTO), whose policies could mean starvation for three billion peasant farmers, according to Samir Amin, director of the Third World Forum in Senegal. Unable to grow foodstuffs that can compete with products imported from advanced countries, how can these people survive? When Kyung Hae Lee, a Korean farmer, committed suicide at this year's [2003] WTO meeting in Cancún, Mexico, he was protesting a deadly greed that should enrage us all. His suicide was a desperate call for more of the activist commitment that fills the pages of *Women Writing Resistance*.

The book is a collective "Declaration of Resistance" to the power and arrogance of ruling-class, racist, patriarchal domination. Its call for resistance also imagines a transformed world. These women offer visions that are profoundly revolutionary, and they do so with great beauty. In offering this wealth of prose and poetry by some of the world's finest writers and strongest feminists, Jennifer Browdy confirms that politics and art cannot be separated, despite the critics who try to do so.

Finally, Browdy offers us a shining, elegant introduction that makes the totality of her anthology a work of art in itself. Gracias, Jennifer, *y venceremos*!

WRITING RESISTANCE, ENVISIONING THE BETTER WORLD THAT COULD BE

– Jennifer Browdy –

WOMEN WRITING RESISTANCE: Essays on Latin America and the Caribbean chronicles a time of intense awareness of the effects of globalization—the transnational movements of capital and of people—and of a heightened awareness of the porousness of borders that used to seem firm, especially national and cultural borders. Old categories such as "First World" and "Third World" are no longer neatly mappable, and the old divides of nationality, language, and race have become much more fluid. The contributors to *Women Writing Resistance* range across all these borders, locating themselves in the borderlands between "Latin America," "the Caribbean," and "North America," even as they call into question the validity of such labels as signposts to identity.

From Latinas of various national origins, many now writing in exile, to writers of Anglophone and Francophone Caribbean origins, to members of the Hispanic Jewish diaspora, to Chicanas who culturally straddle the US-Mexico border, to Puertorriqueñas with their special hybrid American political status, and even including one North American of European Jewish ancestry, Margaret

Randall, whose lifetime of commitment to social justice movements in Mexico, Cuba, Nicaragua, and North America make her an inveterate border crosser—the contributors to *Women Writing Resistance* exemplify the possibility of coalition and alliance among women from widely divergent backgrounds, all working in what Aurora Levins Morales calls the field of "cultural activism" to envision and manifest a more equitable, peaceful, and sustainable future for the Americas and the world.[1]

Beyond their commitment to social justice, the authors included in *Women Writing Resistance* are outstanding writers, garnering international acclaim for their novels, poetry, and essays, which often make use of formal innovations such as linguistic code switching, oral history, authorial collaboration, and the creative juxtaposition of previously "pure" genres such as poetry and prose or fiction and nonfiction, all in the service of textualizing previously marginalized, culturally complex voices. All the contributors have enacted in their writing what Mary K. DeShazer has called "a poetics of resistance," in which writers "participate in resistance by inscribing it" in beautiful, powerful poetry and prose.[2]

To understand these writers' resistant politics, we must explore the history of Latin America and the Caribbean, which forms the backdrop of their work. Globalization as a socio-historical phenomenon has been going on for a long time: it began to assume its current configuration roughly five hundred years ago, when the age of European imperialist domination of the peoples of Africa, Asia, the Middle East, and the Americas began. This Euro-American cultural hegemony has always been accompanied by various kinds of resistance movements. In Latin America and the Caribbean, the initial goals of resistance were to throw off the twin yokes of colonization and slavery, goals that were for the most part accomplished by the mid-twentieth century.

But the eradication of slavery and the arrival of nationalist and independence movements did not do much to improve conditions for women and other racial/cultural minorities, or for the poor in general, throughout the region. Social codes that privileged light skin (as evidence of European ancestry) persisted, and women continued to be confined to restricted areas of the patriarchal compound, pinned down by the male supremacist code known as *machismo*.

Not surprisingly, the glaring inequalities of this social system offered many opportunities for oppositional movements to thrive. Socialism was the most widespread social justice movement of the twentieth century in Latin America and the Caribbean. Marxist and Maoist organizers fanned out across the region, spreading a new gospel of egalitarian human rights that attracted a wide following among the millions of disenfranchised, and also stimulated vicious reprisals from conservative leaders, who were supported by the United States in their efforts to maintain power and privilege, under the guise of "fighting the spread of Communism."

During the twenty years between 1965 and 1985, much of Latin America and the Caribbean became an ideological and physical battlefield, with the Cold War between the United States and Soviet Union driving local stakes even higher. Hundreds of thousands of lives were lost; thousands of followers of social justice movements were rounded up, tortured, and "disappeared"; entire families and even villages were dislocated and forced into political exile; and economies were left in ruins, all in the name of "ensuring democracy"—an increasingly obvious euphemism for "securing safe conditions for imperialist capitalism" throughout Latin America, the Caribbean, and other developing regions of the world.[3]

It was in the crucible of this violent, tumultuous period in Latin American and Caribbean history that the women writers included in this collection came of age and developed what Chela Sandoval would call their "oppositional consciousness."[4] Contributors like Marjorie Agosín, Emma Sepúlveda, Julia Alvarez, and Ruth Behar were caught up as children or young adults in the political upheavals of Chile, Argentina, the Dominican Republic, and Cuba, and were driven into exile in the United States, where they continued from afar their commitment to social justice in their countries of origin. *Women Writing Resistance* is especially fortunate to include contributions from three generations of women in the Partnoy family: Alicia Partnoy, who was "disappeared" and tortured in the late 1970s during the Argentinian genocide, an ordeal she chronicled in her book *The Little School*; her mother, Raquel Partnoy, whose essay describes how she channeled her pain at her family's persecution into her painting; and Alicia's daughter Ruth Irupé Sanabria, who was two years old when her mother was "disappeared" and who fled with her parents to the United States after their release from political imprisonment. The generational movement of the Partnoys is emblematic of the collection as a whole, which spans more than thirty years of women's active involvement in resistance, through writing, to various forms of oppression.

In addition to the larger ideological battles between socialism and capitalism that have torn through Latin America over the past fifty years, many of the contributors to *Women Writing Resistance* have also been intimately involved with the feminist struggle to eliminate sexism and with the indigenous and Black struggles to overcome the entrenched racism of Latin America and the Caribbean—struggles that have been waged within both the socialist and the capitalist camps. Margaret Randall has suggested that the socialist movements in Latin America and the Caribbean were impeded by "the failure to develop an indigenous feminist discourse and vital feminist agenda."[5] That said, Latina feminists have been careful, as Aída Hurtado observes, "about not ranking oppressions which might exclude causes perceived as not central to women's rights." Instead, Hurtado continues, Latina feminists "struggle to incorporate diverse issues without losing the centrality of gender in all their battles."[6] Randall puts it categorically: "If a revolution is unable or unwilling to address the needs of *all* people, it is doomed to failure."[7]

This is a lesson that the writers of this collection have learned through painful experience and immediate observation, in a range of specific geopolitical sites throughout the Americas. As women who understand their writing as a form of resistance to the intertwined and complex oppressions of imperialism, elitism, racism, sexism, and homophobia, they have been practicing transnational, intersectional feminism *avant la letter*, long before these terms became fashionable in the US academy. All the contributors to this volume have challenged borders—linguistic, geographical, social, cultural, ideological—through their writing and in their own lives, and in so doing they have, as Aurora Levins Morales put it, "found a way to affirm our complex realities," which are a mirror of the complex realities of so many women of the Americas. "It is this complexity, this many-sided seeing, this daring to name the uses and practices of power wherever they are found," says Morales, "that is our greatest gift."[8]

Both Randall and Morales have offered a comparison between the individual discrimination and abuse often experienced by women under patriarchy, and the collective oppression perpetrated by the male-dominated social forces of imperialism, with its accompanying racism and elitism. "Individual abuse and collective oppression are not different things," Morales declares. "They are different views of the same creature. . . . Personal abuse is the local eruption of systemic oppression, and oppression is the accumulation of millions of small systemic abuses."[9] In order to heal society at both the local and global level, Morales and Randall agree, "personal wholeness and political health . . . must be rewoven into a single fabric. They cannot be separated," writes Randall.[10]

This "reweaving" is a major goal of the writers included in this anthology, whose writings move from the personal to the political and back again with great fluidity, grace, and power. Located as they are, in what Gloria Anzaldúa calls "the borderlands" between cultures, moving back and forth between their "home" countries and their various locations in exile, these writers are all profoundly *mestizo*, to use Anzaldúa's influential term. As Anzaldúa explains:

> The work of mestizo consciousness is to break down the subject-object duality that keeps her a prisoner and to show in the flesh and through the images in her work how duality is transcended. The answer to the problem between the white race and the colored, between males and females, lies in healing the split that originates in the very foundations of our lives, our culture, our languages, our thoughts. A massive uprooting of dualistic thinking in the individual and collective consciousness is the beginning of a long struggle, but one that could, in our best hopes, bring us to the end of rape, of violence, of war.[11]

Undoing the artificial separations between us and them, self and other, has been the project of many postcolonial writers, who have sought to enact a mobile, contingent, strategic deployment of identity in the interests of a politics of solidarity across differences. The writers in *Women Writing Resistance* have all used their writing in the service of what Chela Sandoval calls "global decolonizing alliances," motivated by the goals of "egalitarian social relations and economic well-being for all citizenry"—and also, I would add, for those whose very claim to citizenship is contested, as in the case of Guatemalan Quiché Indian Rigoberta Menchú.[12]

Menchú, who won the Nobel Peace Prize in 1992 for her work as an indigenous human rights leader, chronicled in her best-selling testimonial *I, Rigoberta Menchú*, emerged as an international leader in global struggles for indigenous rights, work that culminated in the 2007 ratification by the United Nations of the Universal Declaration of the Rights of Indigenous Peoples. Menchú has been at the forefront of efforts to bring to justice the perpetrators of the 1970s genocide against the Guatemalans, and she twice ran for president of Guatemala, the first indigenous person to do so in Latin America. In all of her work, Menchú has endeavored to build solidarity between the different ethnic groups in Guatemala, stressing the importance of alliance to successful movements for social change.

"I believe in community as an alternative way forward, and not simply as a memory of the past," Menchú says. "It is something dynamic. Identity is not just nostalgia for eating tamales. It is holistic, and comprises all the integral aspects of a culture."[13] Menchú envisions a new kind of world community, which would be "pluralistic, diverse, multiethnic and multicultural. We must accept that humanity is a beautiful multi-colored garden," she says, using a characteristically organic metaphor.[14]

There is undeniably a current of rage that runs through the writings included in this volume—rage at social injustice, at political oppression, at the collusion of the United States and Europe in sustaining the deep inequities that mar living conditions for the majority throughout Latin America and the Caribbean—and there is also a profound current of sorrow. "My poems acknowledge those voices muzzled in dark and silent torture chambers, especially the voices of women and of children who were forbidden to sing and denied the opportunity to grow knowing the soothing touch of a parent or to simply gaze, unafraid, at open horizons," says Marjorie Agosín.[15] Through remembrance, Agosín, Edwidge Danticat, and others in this collection seek to bear witness to the repressive political regimes of the Americas and to pay homage to those whose lives have been lost unnecessarily. Most of all, these women writers seek to channel their anger, sorrow, and pain in positive directions, undertaking, according to Aurora Levins Morales, "the work of infusing people's imaginations with possibility, with the belief in a bigger future." This cultural activism, she says, "is the essential fuel of revolutionary fire."[16]

The social visions of these women writers are nothing short of revolutionary, demanding a rethinking of history as well as a re-envisioning of the present. Running throughout is an insistence on centering the histories, priorities, and self-determination of all women, but especially women who find themselves disenfranchised and marginalized under patriarchal capitalism. Though the women writers in this collection come from a wide range of cultural, educational, and material circumstances—some having enjoyed positions of relative power and comfort by virtue of their European ancestry, others having been discriminated against on the basis of class or race. But all insist on a radical politics of inclusion, based on what Jacqui Alexander and Chandra Talpade Mohanty describe as "the feminist democratic practice," which calls for solidarity among women across the bounds of nationality, sexuality, race, class, language, ethnicity, religion, and other artificial barriers. As Alexander and Mohanty elaborate:

> In order for solidarity between Third World women in the geographical Third World and women of color in the first world to take place [and, I would add, between the aforementioned groups and white feminists as well] imperialist domination and capitalist attitudes towards acquisition and advancement must become part of a feminist project of liberation. Feminist democratic practice in this context, then, cannot be about self-advancement, upward mobility or maintenance of the

first-world status quo. It has to be premised on the decolonization of the self and on notions of citizenship defined not just within the boundaries of the nation-state, but across national and regional borders.[17]

This collection has grown out of my own experience as a crosser of borders—linguistic, national, racial, and religious, among others—and my ever-growing conviction that if North American feminists want to improve our world, we must begin by reaching beyond the bounds of our own privilege in order to learn from our sisters in struggle in other parts of the globe. I have learned so much as a feminist activist throughout my years of reading and interacting with my Latina and Caribeña counterparts, and it is my vision that this collection will stimulate other North American students of Latin American and Caribbean culture to explore this rich field of cultural knowledge and literary production further, in order to begin to see the world through a radically different lens than that offered by mainstream media, academia, and publishing. Linked in solidarity, we may dare, alongside the writers included in this anthology, to envision a new, people-centered global society, what Alexander and Mohanty call "a transborder participatory democracy (one in which it is not the state but the people themselves who emerge as the chief agents in defining the course of the global economic and political processes that structure their lives)."[18] As always, in order to manifest such a vision, we need our writers and other artists to show us the way, and it is my hope that this collection will be another signpost on the road to a more just world for us all.

As we move through the second decade of the twenty-first century, democracy, human rights, and social justice are once again under threat by the forces of corruption, greed, and repressive political ideologies. In our time, as in the past, "poetry is not a luxury," as Audre Lorde knew so well; "it is a vital necessity of our existence."[19] And a revolutionary poem, as Adrienne Rich observed, "is an alchemy through which waste, greed, brutality, frozen indifference, blind sorrow and anger are transmuted into some drenching recognition of the What if?—the possible. . . . Revolutionary art dwells, by its nature, on edges. . . . This is its power: the tension between subject and means, between the *is* and what can be."[20]

The writers of *Women Writing Resistance* all dwell on that dangerous cutting edge of possibility, stringing out bridges of words into the uncharted future, their writing conjuring what Rich calls "the energy of desire, summoning a different reality,"[21] and calling on us as readers to work with them to create a better world.

NOTES

1. Aurora Levins Morales, *Medicine Stories: History, Culture and the Politics of Integrity* (Cambridge, MA: South End Press, 1998), 4.

2. Mary K. DeShazer, *A Poetics of Resistance: Women Writing in El Salvador, South Africa and the United States* (Ann Arbor: University of Michigan Press, 1994), 311.

3. During the same period, the Chicano/a farmworkers' movement waged a similar ideological battle for better working conditions within the United States but were perceived as less threatening than the openly Communist *campesinos* in countries such as Guatemala, El Salvador, and Chile, and were thus treated with somewhat more respect than their counterparts in Central and South America.

4. Chela Sandoval, *Methodology of the Oppressed* (Minneapolis: University of Minnesota Press, 2000), 43.

5. Margaret Randall, *Gathering Rage: The Failure of Twentieth-Century Revolutions to Develop a Feminist Agenda* (New York: Monthly Review Press, 1992), 160.

6. Aída Hurtado, "*Sitios y Lenguas:* Chicanas Theorize Feminism" in *Decentering the Center: Philosophy for a Multicultural, Postcolonial, and Feminist World*, ed. Uma Narayan and Sandra G. Harding (Bloomington: Indiana University Press, 2000).

7. Randall, *Gathering Rage*, op. cit., 171.

8. Morales, *Medicine Stories*, op. cit., 65.

9. Ibid., 4.

10. Randall, *Gathering Rage*, op. cit., 164.

11. Gloria Anzaldúa, *Borderlands/La frontera* (San Francisco: Spinsters/ Aunt Lute, 1987), 80.

12. Sandoval, *Methodology of the Oppressed*, op. cit., 182.

13. Rigoberta Menchú, *Crossing Borders*, trans. and ed. Ann Wright (London: Verso, 1998), 223.

14. Ibid., 221.

15. Marjorie Agosín, *An Absence of Shadows*, trans. Celeste Kostopulos-Cooperman, Cola Franzen, and Mary G. Berg (Fredonia, NY: White Pine Press, 1998), 11.

16. Morales, *Medicine Stories*, op. cit., 4.

17. M. Jacqui Alexander and Chandra Talpade Mohanty, "Introduction: Genealogies, Legacies, Movements," in *Feminist Genealogies, Colonial Legacies, Democratic Futures*, ed. M. Jacqui Alexander and Chandra Talpade Mohanty (New York: Routledge, 1997), xli.

18. Ibid.

19. Audre Lorde, *Sister Outsider: Essays and Speeches* (Freedom, CA: Crossing Press, 1984), 37.

20. Adrienne Rich, *What Is Found There: Notebooks on Poetry and Politics* (New York: W. W. Norton, 1993), 241–42.

21. Ibid., 242.

PART ONE

RE-ENVISIONING HISTORY

1

REVISION

– Aurora Levins Morales –

LET'S GET ONE THING STRAIGHT. Puerto Rico was a women's country. We outnumbered men again and again.[1] Female head of household is not a new thing with us. The men left for Mexico and Venezuela and Peru. They left every which way they could, and they left us behind. We got our own rice and beans. Our own *guineo verde* and cornmeal. Whatever there was to be cooked, we cooked it. Whoever was born, we birthed and raised them. Whatever was to be washed, we washed it. We washed the ore the men dug from the mountains, rinsed a thousand baskets of crushed rock. We stood knee deep in the rivers, separating gold from sand, and still cooked supper. We washed cotton shirts and silk capes, diapers and menstrual cloths, dress shirts and cleaning rags. We squatted by the river and pounded clothing on rocks. Whatever was grown, we grew it. We planted the food and harvested it. We pushed the cane into the teeth of the trapiche and stripped the tobacco leaf from the stem. We coaxed the berries from the coffee branch and sorted them, washed them, dried them, shelled them, roasted them, ground them, made the coffee, and served it. We were never still, our hands were always busy. Making soap. Making candles. Holding children. Making bedding. Sewing clothing. Our stitches held sleeve to dress and soul to body. We stitched our families through the dead season of the cane, stitched them through lean times of bread and coffee. The seams we made kept us from freezing in the winters of New York and put beans on the table in the years of soup kitchens. Puerto Rican women have always held up four-fifths of the sky. Ours is the work they decided to call unwork. The tasks as necessary as air. Not a single thing they did could have been done without us. Not a treasure taken. Not a crop brought in. Not a town built up around its plaza, not a fortress manned without our cooking, cleaning, sewing, laundering, childbearing. We have always been here, doing what had to be done. As reliable as furniture, as supportive as their favorite *sillón*. Who thanks his bed? But we are not furniture. We are full of fire, dreams, pain, subversive laughter. How could they not honor us? We were always here, working, eating, sleeping, singing, suffering, giving birth, dying. We were out of their sight, cutting wood, making fire, soaking beans, nursing babies. We were right there beside them digging, hoeing, weeding, picking, cutting, stacking. Twisting wires, packing *piña*, shaping pills, filling thermometers with poisonous metal, typing memo after memo. Not one meal was ever eaten without our hand on the pot. Not one office ran for an hour without our ear to the phone, our finger to the keyboard. Not one of those books that ignore us could have been written without our shopping, baking, mending, ironing, typing, making coffee, comforting. Without our caring for the children, minding the store, getting in the crop, making their businesses pay. This is *our* story, and the truth of our lives will overthrow them.

Let's get one thing straight. Puerto Rico was *parda, negra, mulata, mestiza*. Not a country of Spaniards at all. We outnumbered them, year after year. All of us who are written down: not white. We were everywhere. Not just a few docile servants and the guava-eating ghosts of the dead. The Spanish men left babies right and left. When most of the Indias had given birth to mixed-blood children, when all the lands had been divided, our labor shared out in *encomienda*, and no more caciques went out to battle them, they said the people were gone. How could we be gone? We were the brown and olive and cream-colored children of our mothers: Arawak, Maya, Lucaya, stolen women from all the shores of the sea. When we cooked, it was the food our mothers had always given us. We still pounded yuca and caught crabs. We still seasoned our stews with aji and wore cotton skirts. When we burned their fields, stole their cattle, set fire to their boats, they said we were someone else. What was wrong with their eyes? We mixed our blood together like *sancocho, calald*. But the mother things stayed with us. Two hundred and fifty years after they said, "*Ya no hay Indios*," we had a town of two thousand who still remembered our names, and even our neighbors called the place Indiera. When they wanted more slaves from Africa, they complained that we had all died on them. They called us *pardas libres* and stopped counting us. Invisibility is not a new thing with us. But we have always been here, working, eating, sleeping, singing, suffering, giving birth, dying. We are not a metaphor. We are not ghosts. We are still here.

Let's get one thing straight. We were everywhere. The Spanish, Dutch, English, French, Genoese, Portuguese took captives up and down our coasts, inland by river, overland on foot. They brought us here through every bay deep enough to hold a slave ship. Legally, through the port of San Juan, all registered in the royal books. And dozens more, unloaded at night, right there in the harbor, sold but not written down. But that was the least of it. We came through Añasco, Guinica, Arecibo, Salinas, San German. In sloops from Jamaica, St. Christopher, Curacao. We came by the thousands, bound hand and foot, uncounted, unaccounted for, while official eyes looked the other way. And we came as fugitives from the other islands, because the Spanish let the slaves of their rivals live here free. From Saint Croix and Tortola, from Jamaica and the Virgins.

There were many more of us than were written in their registers. Untaxed, unbaptised, hidden in the folds of the mountains, in the untitled lands. There were many more of us than the sugar planters knew or would say, always sobbing to the king about no one to do the work. We were here from the start, and we were here more often. They were always running away to seek better fortunes. We ran away, too. We ran to the swamps and we ran to the *cordillera*. We ate their cattle and set fire to their cane fields. If they caught us, the judges were instructed to cut off our ears. (Police brutality is not a new thing with us.) Spanish men left babies right and left, *cafe con leche* children. But in their imaginations, they were all alone in their big white houses, dreaming of Peru or the voyage back to Spain, while on their threshold a new people was forming. How could they not see us, nursing their babies, cooking *fiame*, frying balls of cornmeal, banana, yuca; stewing up crabs and pork and *guingambo*. Wrapping cotton rags around our heads. Throwing white flowers into the sea. How could they not hear us, telling each other our stories with the soles of our feet on the clay, with the palms of our hands on tree trunks, on goat-hides. Carrying their loads, laundering for strangers to earn them cash. We have always been here, longer and steadier, working, eating, sleeping, singing, suffering, giving birth, dying. We were not contented. We were not simple souls ready to dance and sing all day with innocent hearts. We were not lazy animals, too dull-witted to understand orders. We were not hot-blooded savages, eager to be raped. We were not impervious to pain. We felt every blow they struck at our hearts. We were not happy to serve. We didn't love our masters. We were slaves. We were *libertas*. We were free mulatas. We were poor and hungry and alive. When they needed hands, they brought us. When they needed jobs, they threw us on boats to New York and Hawaii, threw us on food stamps, threw us drugs. But Puerto Rico is African. We made it from our own flesh.

Let's get one thing straight. Puerto Rico was a poor folks' country. There were many more poor than rich throughout its history. More *naborias* than *caciques*. More foot soldiers than aristocratic *conquistadores*. More servants than mistresses. More people wearing cotton and leather than people wearing silk and damask, velvet and cloth of gold. They did wear those things, and they ate off silver plates. But most of us ate off *higueras*, or wooden trenchers, or common clay. There were more people who ate *plitano* and cornmeal and *casabe* every day of the week, with a little salt fish or pork now and then, than those who had beef and turtle and chicken and fresh eggs and milk, with Canarias wine and Andalucian olive oil. Most of us had no money. Many of us were never paid for working. Those of us who owned the fruits of our labor traded it to the merchants for far less than it was worth, and bought on credit, and ended up in debt. We were the ones who cleared the land so it could be planted with sugarcanes from India, and coffee bushes from Ethiopia, and bananas and plantains from Malaysia. We were the ones who grew food. We were the ones who were glad when a store came to the mountains, and then watched our future harvests promised for the sack of beans, the new blade, the bag of rice or corn meal. We were the hands of Pietri and Castañer. We were the hands of Ferré and Muñoz. We washed and ironed the shirts of the politicians. We scrubbed the pots of the governors and their wives. We sewed those fine christening gowns for their babies and fetched the water for their baths. They said, This governor built a wall, and that one made a road. They said so-and-so founded a town, and this other one produced a newspaper. But the governor did not lift blocks of stone or dig through the thick clay. The *capitanes pobladores* didn't labor in childbed to populate their villas, or empty the chamber pots. The great men of letters didn't carry the bales of paper or scrub ink from piles of shirts and trousers. We have always been here. How could they not see us? We filled their plates and made their beds, washed their clothing and made them rich. We were not mindless, stupid, created for the tasks we were given. We were tired and angry and alive. How could they miss us? We were the horses they rode, we were the wheels of their family pride. We were the springs where they drank, and our lives went down their throats. Our touch was on every single thing they saw. Our voices were around them humming, whispering, singing, telling riddles, making life in the dust and mud. We have always been here, doing what had to be done, working, eating, sleeping, singing, suffering, giving birth, dying. Dying of hunger and parasites, of cholera and tuberculosis. Dying of typhus and anemia and cirrhosis of the liver. Dying of heroin and crack and botched abortions, in childbirth and industrial accidents, and from not enough days off. This is our history. We met necessity every single day of our lives. Look wherever you like, it's our work you see.

NOTES

1. This was not true in many times and places. Overall, there were more male than female slaves, for example. But in San Juan, women often outnumbered men, notably in the 1600s and in the slave population just before emancipation; also possibly among rural subsistence farmers in the mountain regions.

2

WE ARE UGLY,
BUT WE ARE HERE

– Edwidge Danticat –

ONE OF THE FIRST people murdered on our land was a queen. Her name was Anacaona, and she was an Arawak Indian. She was a poet, dancer, and even a painter. She ruled over the western part of an island so lush and green that the Arawaks called it Ayiti, land of high. When the Spaniards came from across the sea to look for gold, Anacaona was one of their first victims. She was raped and killed and her village pillaged. Anacaona's land is now often called the poorest country in the Western Hemisphere, a place of continuous political unrest. Thus, for some, it is easy to forget that this land was the first black republic, home to the first people of African descent to uproot slavery and create an independent nation in 1804.

I was born under Haiti's dictatorial Duvalier regime. When I was four, my parents left Haiti to seek a better life in the United States. I must admit that their motives were more economic than political, but as anyone who knows Haiti will tell you, economics and politics are intrinsically related; who is in power determines to a great extent whether or not people will eat.

I am thirty-four years old now and have spent more than two-thirds of my life in the United States. My most vivid childhood memories of Haiti involve sudden power failures, "blakawouts," we called them. During blackouts, I couldn't read, study, or watch television, so I'd sit around a candle or a kerosene lamp and listen to stories from the elders in the house.

My grandmother was an old country woman who always felt displaced in the capital where we lived. She had nothing but her patched-up quilts and her stories to console her. She was the one who told me about Anacaona. I used to share a room with her, and I was in the room with her when she died. She was over a hundred years old. She died with her eyes wide open; I was the one who closed them. I still miss the countless stories she told us. However, I accepted her death very easily because death was always around.

As a little girl, I attended more than my share of funerals. My uncle and legal guardian was a Baptist minister and his family was expected to attend every funeral he presided over. I went to all the funerals in the same white lace dress. Perhaps it was because I attended so many funerals that I have such a strong feeling that death is not the end, that the people we put in the ground are going off to live somewhere else. But at the same time I believe they will always hover around to watch over us and guide us through our journeys.

When I was eight, my uncle's brother-in-law went on a long journey to cut cane in the Dominican Republic. He came back deathly ill. I remember his wife twirling feathers inside his nostrils and rubbing black pepper on his upper lip to make him sneeze. She strongly believed that if he sneezed, he would live. At night, it was my job to watch the sky above the house for signs of falling stars. In rural Haitian lore, when a star falls out of the sky, it means someone will die. A star did fall out of the sky and he did die.

I have childhood memories of Jean-Claude "Baby Doc" Duvalier and his wife, Michèle, racing by in their Mercedes-Benz and throwing money out the window to the very poor children in our neighborhood. The children would nearly kill each other trying to catch a coin or a glimpse of Baby Doc and Michèle. One Christmas, it was announced on the radio that the First Lady would be giving away free toys at the palace. My cousins and I went to the palace and were nearly crushed in the mob of children who flooded the palace lawns.

These stories and memories bring the questions always buzzing to my head. What is my place now in all of this? What was my grandmother's place? What is the legacy of the daughters of Anacaona, the daughters of Haiti?

Watching the news reports, it is often hard to tell whether there are real living and breathing women in conflict-stricken places like Haiti. The evening news broadcasts only allow us brief glimpses of presidential coups, rejected boat people, and sabotaged elections. The women's stories never manage to make the front page. But they do exist.

Over the years, I have known women who, when the soldiers came to their homes in Haiti, would tell their children to lie still and play dead. I once met a woman whose sister was shot in her pregnant stomach because she was wearing a T-shirt with an "antimilitary image." I know a mother who was arrested and beaten for working with a pro-democracy group. Her body remains laced with scars where the soldiers put out their cigarettes on her flesh. At night, this woman still smells the ashes of cigarette butts that were stuffed, lit, inside her nostrils. In the same jail cell, this woman watched as paramilitary attachés raped her fourteen-year-old daughter at gunpoint. When mother and daughter took a tiny boat to the United States, the mother had no idea that her daughter was pregnant. Nor did she know that her child had gotten the HIV virus from one of the paramilitary men who had raped her. The offspring of the rape, her grandchild, was named Anacaona after the Arawak queen, because that family of women is from Léogane, the same region where Anacaona was murdered, the same region where my grandmother was born.

The infant Anacaona has a face which no longer shows any trace of indigenous blood, but her story echoes some of the first incidents of bloodshed in a land that has seen so much more than its share.

There is a Haitian saying that might upset the aesthetic sensibilities of some women. "*Nou lèd, nou la,*" it says. "We are ugly, but we are here." Like the modesty that is common in rural Haitian culture, this saying makes a deeper claim for poor Haitian women than maintaining beauty, be it skin-deep or otherwise. For women like my grandmother, what is worth celebrating is the fact that we are here, that against all the odds, we exist. To women like my grandmother, who greeted each other with this saying when they met along a trail in the countryside, the very essence of life lies in survival. It is always worth reminding our sisters that we have lived yet another day to answer the roll call of an often painful and very difficult life. It is in this spirit that to this day a woman remembers to name her child Anacaona, a name which resonates both the splendor and agony of a past that haunts so many women, and men, today.

When they were enslaved, our foremothers believed that when they died their spirits would return to Africa, most specifically to a peaceful land we call Ginen, where gods and goddesses live. The women who came before me were women who spoke half of one language and half another. They spoke the French and Spanish of their colonizers mixed in with their own African language. These women seemed to be speaking in tongues when they prayed to their old gods, the ancient African spirits. Even though they were afraid that their old deities would no longer understand them, they invented a new language with which to describe their new surroundings, a language from which colorful phrases blossomed to fit the desperate circumstances. When these women greeted each other, they found themselves speaking in codes.

—How are we today, sister?

—I am ugly, but I am here.

These days, many of my sisters are greeting each other far away from the lands where they first learned to speak in tongues. Many have made it to other shores, after traveling endless miles on the high seas, on rickety boats that almost took their lives. On October 29, 2002, a woman, weakened by a long ocean journey, spotted land and leapt into the shallow tide. Others followed, including little girls and boys who risked breaking an arm or a leg rather than separate from their parents. These are only some of the thousands who reach American shores each year, only to be rounded up, shackled, and taken away, often sent back where they came from. Eleven years ago, a mother jumped into the sea when she discovered that her baby daughter had died in her arms on a journey that she had hoped would take them to a brighter future. Mother and child, they sank to the bottom of an ocean which already holds millions of souls from the middle passage, the holocaust of the slave trade. That woman's sacrifice moved many of us to tears, even while it reminded us of a slew of past sacrifices made previously for all of us, so that we could be here.

The past is full of examples of our foremothers showing such deep trust in the sea that they would jump off slave ships and let the waves embrace them. They believed that the sea was the beginning and the end of all things, the road to freedom and their entrance to Ginen. These women, women like my grandmother who had taught me the story of Anacaona, the queen, have been part of the very construction of my being ever since I was a little girl.

My grandmother believed that if a life is lost, then another one springs up replanted somewhere else, the next life even stronger

than the last. She believed that no one really dies as long as someone remembers, someone who will acknowledge that this person
had, in spite of everything, been here. We are part of an endless
circle, the daughters of Anacaona. We have stumbled, but have not
fallen. We are ill-favored, but still we endure. Every once in a while,
we must scream this as far as the wind can carry our voices. "Nou
lèd, nou la!" We are ugly, but we are here!

And here to stay.

3

THE SILENT WITNESS

– Raquel Partnoy –

MY GRANDPARENTS WERE Russian-Jewish immigrants who settled in Argentina in 1913, shortly before World War I. They decided to leave their country because of Czarist persecution and discrimination against the Jewish people. My father arrived with part of his family; the ones who remained in Russia died during the war. My mother went with twenty-four family members, including her uncle and his family. They were not able to pack many of their belongings, but they did bring with them a samovar, a mandolin, and a sewing machine. In their new country they began to rebuild their lives, always preserving their traditions, language, and cultural heritage. It was not a difficult task, since they lived in a Jewish settlement.

Both my parents arrived in their teenage years. Later, they met, got married, and moved to Rosario—the second biggest Argentinian city. There they built a house in a neighborhood populated mostly by immigrants from Italy and Spain, with a few others from Russia and Arabia. I was born in that house when my two brothers were ten and fifteen years old. Although my parents and my only living grandfather used to speak to us in Yiddish, we answered in Spanish. When my parents and their neighbors from different countries met, they would speak in strongly accented Spanish.

My mother set the samovar on a little table, over a starched, crocheted mat, but no longer used it for making tea. Its shining bronze body became very familiar to me. It was funny to see my face, distorted and multiplied, reflected on it. The family album was on the shelf behind that table. The faces of children with adult expressions looked at me from a distant time and place. Many of those pictures had been taken in Russia. For years I looked at those photos over and over, always trying to catch a glimpse of the life experiences of the relatives portrayed there.

Although my father used to play the mandolin in Russia, I never heard him play it again in Argentina. Maybe he was too busy making a living. He then gave me the stringless mandolin as a toy. I can remember the feeling when I slid my hands over its soft wooden belly. Later, I fixed it with old strings to hear its sound.

However, it was my oldest brother, not me, who inherited a musical vocation. At a very young age he became a violin teacher and later on he joined a popular orchestra. I was a child when the musicians, also children of immigrants, came to rehearse in the patio of our house. During the summertime, the grapevines hung like a ceiling above us. Surrounded by the high palm tree and plants of all shapes, the orchestra played tangos. Upon hearing the first sounds, our neighbors' children came to enjoy the music with us.

All those evenings remain strongly etched in my memory. In fact almost every remembrance I have from my childhood is related to the patio of that house. It was there that I began to draw with white chalk on the green zinc wall of the kitchen. I loved that large space where I could spend many hours looking for different shapes. When I finished, I would simply erase my drawings with wet rags to start again.

One of my brothers gave me his watercolors. That used box of colors was a treasure for me since I had never owned any painting supplies. I began painting on the blank side of large printed papers I had gotten somewhere at home. Maybe I would have been happier with a variety of art supplies, like today's children, but at that time, parents did not buy many toys, coloring pencils, or paintings for their children.

In the summers I enjoyed helping my mother wash the tiles of the patio and water the plants. I remember lying barefoot on those hot afternoons, on the still wet and fresh granite tiles beneath the long corridor. I would look at the countless tiny particles in the tiles and discover shapes and colors.

An oil landscape, painted by a family friend, was hung on the wall of the corridor. It showed a row of green cypresses cut out against a discolored blue sky. I remember its details not because I liked it, but because it was the only painting I had ever seen. A long time would have to pass until I could finally see the original works of a good artist.

By the time I was five years old, my brothers were fifteen and twenty. I grew up like an only child. My brothers used to spend time with me; they took me to the movies, to the park, or to the river, which I enjoyed very much. It was, however, like having two extra fathers. I used to wander around the house trying to entertain myself. I usually ended up knocking at the high doors of the rooms by the corridor, asking the people I imagined living there if they would buy fabrics. I recall the pleasant feeling of their diverse textures on the tip of my fingers. Many years later I went back to fabrics, using them in my paintings.

ART AND LIFE

Looking back, I can see that all the series I painted reflect both my heritage and my own experiences. When my parents grew older they gave me the samovar because, according to the Jewish tradition, it has to be left to the youngest child. The samovar came to my home with all the family memories, and I decided to preserve them in my paintings.

My mother also gave me the family album. Cracked old photographs with strange and sad faces, nostalgic brides with forced smiles, baby girls with huge topknots, baby boys lying over embroidered sheets, showing their naked behinds. There was also the picture of my elegant uncle Simon, a tailor; another of my grandfather Moises, the rabbi; my grandmother Raquel with her beautiful face and a shawl over her head. All those photographs told me stories, stories about generations that come and generations that go. They spoke of life, exile, and death. I used those stories to paint my series *From Life, Life's Windows,* and *The Brides.*

When working on these paintings, not only was I interested in preserving my family memories, but also in portraying both the positive and negative aspects of life. During the years to come I would have to go through more negative than positive events. My series *Life Experiences* is related to the dictatorship in Argentina, when more than 30,000 people "disappeared." Many youth whose only crime was a belief in justice were arrested, tortured, and eventually killed by the authorities. In that series I tell of my own pain for the disappearance and subsequent imprisonment of Alicia, my only daughter.

As the mother of a "disappeared" child I experienced the horror of seeing how my family was gradually destroyed. From the day my daughter and her husband were kidnapped by the military forces, life was not the same for my husband, my son, or myself. Anguish, hatred, and depression overwhelmed us while we wondered if they were still alive, felt impotence because the military wouldn't give us any kind of information, spent endless nights without sleeping for fear that the evil ones would come to our house to take another family member. Those feelings were to destroy our lives forever.

After being disappeared for five months in a concentration camp, enduring all kinds of physical and psychological torture, my daughter and Carlos, my son-in-law, were transferred to different prisons, where they remained for three years. Once in jail, political prisoners were treated more rigorously than dangerous criminals, while their families endured humiliation and discrimination from prison personnel, and were subjected to a severe visiting regime.

My little granddaughter Ruth was eighteen months old when her parents were kidnapped. Her father was taken from his workplace. Ruth was with her mother at home when a large group of armed soldiers arrived. It was noontime. They did not allow neighbors to stay outside and the block was closed to traffic. After knocking at the door of my daughter's house insistently, the soldiers began hitting it brutally, while announcing very loudly that they were the army. When my daughter heard them, she thought about the people who were being disappeared at the time and immediately began to run away, climbing a back wall. They shot at her from a neighbor's roof.

While Alicia was caught, Ruth, who witnessed everything, was crying, terrified. Unlike many other children of the disappeared, who were often stolen from their families, Ruth was left by the soldiers in a neighbor's house. Due to this sad episode, however, she remained vulnerable to loud noises for a long time and was frightened at the sight of people in uniform. I still remember her voice while she wandered around our house knocking at every door, including the refrigerator, asking, "Mami, are you in there?" She would not leave me alone with my sorrows. When I went to my bedroom and closed the door, she used to call me and say, "Come on, let's play!" Ruth lived with us for three years until my husband and I, after presenting requests to many embassies in Buenos Aires, got political asylum for her parents in the United States. They were released from jail and traveled with her to that country.

At the beginning of our odyssey we did not know that we were not alone. Many parents, like us, were going through the nightmare of trying to find out where our children had been taken. We had gone to police stations and army posts; we had talked to priests and military chaplains; we had asked friends if they knew of contacts at the clandestine centers who would be able to say if our children were alive. But the army knew very well how to create a climate of terror in the family of the abducted victim. When Salomon, my husband, went to our city army headquarters to ask about our daughter, they denied she was there and showed him a paper allegedly signed by her, stating that she was released. Where was she then? The scenario of the disappeared was in place, and the creator of this horrible concept, the manager of such a horrendous drama, was the terrorist state of Argentina.

At that time, many families felt miserable, with thousands of young couples disappeared along with their babies or little children. Most of them were murdered by the military forces. During that time I produced the series "Clothes." By painting clothes without people I portrayed the life of Daniel, my only son, who suffered depression during those years, until he could no longer bear it and, at the age of twenty-five, committed suicide.

SECRETS OF THE SAMOVAR

In 1994 Salomon and I moved to Washington, DC, to join our daughter, Alicia, and her family. We brought with us the old family samovar. For many years the samovar has been the silent witness to the lives of our family, traveling from Russia to Argentina and then to the United States. How many familiar faces have been reflected on its shiny surface? How many stories are engraved in its bronze body? After moving to Washington, I went back to the family photos, which I had also brought with me, to find those answers. I began to paint the series entitled *The Secrets of the Samovar*.

It wasn't until I visited the Holocaust Memorial Museum in Washington, DC, in 1995, that I realized my series of paintings about the Jewish people lacked an important component. I began searching the Internet for testimonials and images of Holocaust survivors for my *Surviving Genocide* series. While reading testimonies, I found these words: "I am now standing at the boundary between life and death. I already know for certain that I must die and that is why I want to bid farewell to my friends and to my work." This farewell message had been left by Gela Seksztajn, an artist born in Warsaw in 1907 and murdered in August 1942 in the Treblinka concentration camp. Her message, along with her watercolor paintings, were preserved underground in the Warsaw ghetto.

She had continued: "Farewell, comrades and friends. Jews! Do everything that such a tragedy will never be repeated!" There on my computer screen, next to her words, was her self-portrait. Looking at the strong lines of her face, the hard expression of her eyebrows, and the rage in her powerful eyes, I felt as if those eyes were staring at future generations, demanding of them that her wishes be fulfilled. Reading her words, I thought about the genocide committed by the military dictatorship in Argentina. "*Do everything that such a tragedy will never be repeated,*" said Gela. "Never again!" are words that every survivor and every family member of a disappeared person in Argentina will repeat forever.

As I began to read survivors' testimonies, I noticed many similarities in procedures between the genocide committed during the Holocaust and that perpetrated by the military dictatorship in Argentina. In both cases the victims were taken from their homes or workplaces by the army or policemen in uniforms or by paramilitary forces in civilian clothes. The perpetrators mostly came at night, but sometimes they acted during the day. While beating up the victims and screaming at them, the attackers destroyed or stole all their belongings. The victims were then kidnapped by their oppressors. After losing everything—their families, their names, and their possessions—the victims were taken to concentration camps where they endured all types of physical and mental torture before being murdered. In the process of dehumanizing prisoners, the military forces did not allow them to use their names. They were identified only by numbers.

For weeks, months, years, their family members were left without knowing anything about their disappeared loved ones. Relatives entered a world of madness where it was impossible to get information from the authorities concerning the whereabouts of their son, their daughter, or their parent. Frequently, several members of the same family were abducted by the military forces; this left the ones who remained at home absolutely helpless.

As in the Holocaust, the majority of the Argentine population remained in silence while the military government committed all kinds of atrocities. Nobody seemed to know what was happening, but when confronted with the facts, people used to say, "They must be guilty of something," as a way to justify such horror.

SURVIVING GENOCIDE

The history of genocide in Argentina has a living and powerful witness: Las Madres de la Plaza de Mayo (The Mothers of the Plaza de Mayo), an organization created during the dictatorship by the mothers of disappeared children. They have been marching every Thursday at the Plaza de Mayo, across the street from the Government House, since April 30, 1977, one year after the military coup. The women carry large signs with the photos of their children and ask for their whereabouts. After twenty-five years they have become a symbol of strength, courage, and resistance around the world. Yet, after so long, the large majority of the perpetrators of such massive human rights violations remain totally unpunished. In 1983, when democracy again returned to Argentina, the government applied amnesty laws and pardoned all those responsible for the murders.

When I began to focus my work on the Jewish people around the European Holocaust, I realized that the reason I understood the Holocaust survivors' testimonies so deeply was because of my own experiences during Argentina's military dictatorship genocide. It was then that I decided to unify both subjects and paint the series *Surviving Genocide*.

I chose a large canvas to start this new series. My first theme was "the message," where I tried to express how any kind of message can threaten or change our lives in a single minute. By painting a couple wrapped in themselves, surrounded by large and small envelopes held by shadowy figures, empty clothes almost flying over their heads, I wanted to portray the constant menace that surrounds individuals as well as family groups, when they live under a totalitarian regime. I took the idea for this painting from an ink drawing I had made in 1982 called *The Message Arrives . . .* which I now regard as a premonition, because it was made one year before I received the news that my son had taken his life.

The unpredictable existence during military rule in Argentina, when people disappeared every day, the uncertainty that many families experienced in their daily lives, created all kinds of horrible feelings, but above all, fear. In fact, fear and death were extremely related during those days. When the military forces, using large numbers of armed soldiers, brutally burst into houses, shouting and breaking windows and doors to grab people, they deliberately generated an atmosphere of terror. Knowing about all the murders and having experienced my daughter's disappearance, it was not strange to have the dream I translated into my painting *Dancing with Death*. I was dancing with my daughter very softly, but, maybe because of my fear that she was already dead, suddenly I realized she was dead in my arms. After twenty-five years I can never forget that dream, and I still have dreams related to those horrible days.

WOMEN OF THE TANGO

I went back to women's issues when I portrayed *Women of the Tango*. I had always liked tango music, but later on I began to pay more attention to tango lyrics, especially to those that were telling women's stories, stories about abuse and discrimination.

The tango is urban music from Buenos Aires. It was born at the end of the nineteenth century. The millions of immigrants who arrived in Argentina at that time created the necessary environment for the beginning of tango. Most of the immigrants, who were poor, settled in Buenos Aires. However, that city was not ready yet to receive such a large number of people. Many unscrupulous persons took advantage of the situation and built precarious buildings with lots of rooms or remodeled big houses from the colonial years. For many years the immigrants, as well as the poor people from Buenos Aires, had to live in those unhealthy tenement buildings, which led to an increase in disease, alcoholism, prostitution, and many other problems. There was also resentment between the native people and the foreigners who wanted to find a place in that society. The working class plunged into sadness and hopelessness. Those were precisely the feelings that gave musicians and poets the inspiration to create tango.

At the beginning tango was a melody, to which, over the years, urban poets began to set lyrics. Those first lyrics tell us about the underworld life, describing characters who lived in the tenement houses. Tango lyrics referred to the *guapo*, who was feared, respected, and envied among the people of the neighborhood because he was courageous and loyal; the *compadrito*, a quarrelsome coward who used to provoke fights just to show off in front of other people; and the *cafischio* (pimp), who did not like working but was fond of the fine clothes, jewelry, and perfume that his exploitation of prostitute women could provide. The stories of young women who were born in crowded tenements and endured poverty were frequently found in tango lyrics. When they were lured with false promises by the pimps, the women worked in cabarets, enduring a life of prostitution and exploitation that was very difficult to escape.

Through many tango lyrics we learn about the ways these women were discriminated against and mistreated by a *machista* society. Sometimes the inspiration for a tango was a real woman who had died very young after a sad life filled with disease and anguish, whose story could only be found in the hospital files. Malena, Madame Ivonne, Ivette, and Margot are some of the historical names I chose to include in my series about the women of the tango.

EPILOGUE

The large number of European immigrants who began to arrive in Argentina more than a century ago brought with them their cultural heritage: language, music, feelings. Those things were part of their legacy to that country, but at the same time they assimilated to Argentine culture. This exchange between cultures gave the country another physiognomy: many foreign words were incorporated into its slang, there was access to music from other countries, and different stories could be heard in its streets. This new human landscape was inherited by the children of the immigrants, whose parents did not have the time or the skills to write their own stories, stories of nostalgia, assimilation, memories.

As a daughter of immigrants I feel deeply connected to my roots, but I also feel close to all those who suffer repression and injustice. I am fortunate to have the samovar in my home to remind me about my grandparents' experiences in Russia and my own in Argentina. This Silent Witness will also keep in its memory the stories of how terrorism and the so-called war on terrorism brought death and destruction in the United States and abroad. It will remember the cruel attacks against the civilian populations of Afghanistan and Iraq. While the samovar resides with me and my descendants, it will serve as a reminder of the ways anger and greed can deprive people of freedom and peace. It will help us resist, it will never let us forget.

4

AND WHAT WOULD
IT BE LIKE?

– Michelle Cliff –

I.

And what would it be like
The terrain of my girlhood

{with you}   There is no map

Ok.

Mangoes
then the sweet liquidity of star apple
custard apple
sweetsop
cut with sharp tamarind
washed down with coconut water
ginep   slippery
papaya
where restless baby-ghosts vent their furies

all devoured
against trade winds
                        Will I eternally return to the Trade?

Then—
there's more
by which I mean
hibiscus, jasmine, night-blooming   and otherwise
by which I mean
the more ancient
pre-Columbian   pre-Contact
growth
edenic underbrush
unyielding   thick as a woman's thatch
like the {girl's school legend} un-drawered tennis mistress
who
or whom
we slid beneath
to glimpse the bright, thick ginger
womanly—
God, we wanted to be women, never knowing what that meant.
—Patch
thatch so thick you'd never guess she was British
our prejudice.

And banana leaves
which are as wide as a girl's waist—sometimes
and as long as a girl's feathered legs
which exude the juice of the fruit
without a taste of the fruit
dependable as any aunt

down a falls once owned by an aunt
we flowed
on the impossible green

into the equally impossible blue
lit by the height of an impossible light
taking our half-naked selves
down the sweet
into the salt
water
and women
women and water
my grandmother's river
my distant aunt's falls
no one else was allowed in
children   that didn't feel right
revolutionaries are made, not born.

II.
Bougainvillea
grows
{in the botanist's term}
in showy profusion—
but scentless—
disappoints.

III.
Under the high-legged mahogany bed
caciques at each corner   like apostles
the tail of a scorpion is set to strike
transparent   dangerous
I know its poison.

IV.
All feels wild from this distance.

V.

Once at Cable Hut
I fell into a sinkhole
down and down and down
but came back up
Once I had my period and swam way out
past the coral reef
and wondered if a shark would be drawn to me
as the warm salt drew the blood out   and the sea roared
Once I speared a lobster clean   underwater at Lime Key
Once I brushed beside the flimsy nightdress
of a jellyfish and have a mark on my leg to prove it
Once I dodged an alligator in a swamp at the Carib's edge
my mouth gorged on a hundred oysters   their grit becoming
pearl against my teeth
Once I played with a cousin's cock underwater
he taught me to shoot coconuts between the eyes so they
rained on the sand   it was the least I could do
Those were the dangerous days
There was nothing to stop us   it seemed

VI.

There is no map
only the most ragged path back   to
my love   so much so
she ended up in the bush

          at a school where such things were
taken very seriously   severely
        and
I was left   missing her   never ceasing
        and
she was watched   for signs

                     and
I was left   alone   missing her   never ceasing
                     and
she was not allowed to write   at least she never did
                     and
I walked the length and breadth of the playing fields
                                   I have never felt so lost
not like that
                     and
I wanted to be dead   that's all

                                   finally
the headmistress and head girl found me
in the stacks
                                   weeping
                                   violently
against spines of biology
                         running into history
I can see myself in the lapsed documentary of memory
                         curled up against books, shelves
salting the sea island cotton of my blouse
                     water tearing down my face, school badge
with cross & crown   & Latin motto
                         my parents were summoned
the word was not spoken
                         I was told to forget everything
I would never see her again   I would never see her again
    except in my mind   and to this day
golden
         they rifled my hiding place
ransacked my words   read me aloud   on the
verandah

in the impossible sun

my father   uttering

"When you're twenty we'll laugh about this."

that I remember

they took me, on the advice of the doctor who delivered me,

to Doctor's Cave

which is a beach, not Prospero's vault.

for weeks

I swam

like Caliban

her feathered legs opening underwater   salt rushing in

I was exhausted, they said

excitable

I wanted to be a wild colonial girl

And for a time, I was.

5

EVERYTHING I KEPT

Reflections of an "Anthropoeta"

– Ruth Behar –

IF I HAD TO CHOOSE one aspect of my life that had the greatest impact on me as a thinker and a writer, it would be that I was born a Jew in Cuba. And after that, it would be that I came to the United States as an immigrant child, carrying this doubled sense of identity which would eventually be articulated in an American context in the English language, but always with a longing for the native Spanish that was spoken in my family. As a girl and a young woman growing up in New York, I struggled to find a way to give voice to the experience of being a Cuban immigrant, while always yearning to know the island that my family remembered nostalgically, but to which I was told we would never again return to live.

Like other young Cubans of my generation who came of age in the United States in the 1960s and 1970s, I was politicized by the leftist and multiculturalist movements of the era. I searched for a way to take pride in my Cuban identity, while trying not to internalize the epithet of being a *gusana*, "a worm of the revolution," as those of us who left Cuba after the revolution of 1959 had been branded. The young Cubans of the era chose the slogan, "Not all Cubans are *gusanos*," and that's how I would have described myself at the time. Later, I refused to see myself in such negative, self-annihilating terms, when I came to understand that such an epithet was part of a long Latin American legacy of disowning and declaring traitorous those who dared leave their homelands for "the other America" across the border. I decided that I would find a way to celebrate my identity as a woman of the diaspora, while still reclaiming my bond with the island that it was my destiny to lose as a child, before I knew what it meant to have a country.

As a girl, I thought that the best vehicle to express my feelings about these complex yearnings would be poetry and fiction, and I went off to college with the hope of becoming a writer. But I soon lost confidence in my voice as an artist. I was, then, the "Obedient Student" of my poem by that name, and when my teachers discouraged my efforts at poetry, I gave it up. Perhaps, ultimately, it was a good thing that I put aside my artistic ambitions, because it was a moment when I was searching for an intellectual framework in which to examine issues of language, culture, and belonging, issues I didn't yet know how to ground in social and political reality. In my last year in college, an inspiring anthropology teacher convinced me I had the potential to become an anthropologist. Following his advice, I decided to turn my creative impulses to the study of anthropology.

Anthropology offered me a crucial intellectual and philosophical framework for my explorations of identity, memory, home, and the crossing of borders, the dislocations that are at the root of anthropological thinking and that are part of the lived experience of those who live in the diaspora. It was through anthropology, as well, that I was able to undertake the magical, and also politicizing, journeys into the everyday reality of people living in the Spanish-speaking world. My anthropology took me to a rural village in northern Spain, a small town in northern Mexico, and eventually, and essentially, back to Cuba, the root of all my wanderings.

I believe that the dreams of our youth never leave us. Even as I tried hard to conform to the norms of academic writing in the discipline, my anthropology became increasingly haunted by my longing for poetry. I told myself I was creating a poetic anthropology, that I was an *anthropoeta*, unveiling the poetic underpinnings of the anthropological quest for home in a world of homelessness and homesickness.

And then, as I began to travel regularly to Cuba beginning eleven years ago, I found myself needing to actually write real poems again. Returning to the homeland I lost as a child made me want to claim poetry again as an essential part of my life. I found that initially, being back in Cuba, I could not do anthropology, I could not speak in the voice I had acquired through my schooling in the United States. I didn't want to turn Cuba into an ethnographic field site. I didn't want to be an anthropologist in Cuba. The experience of being in Cuba was emotionally so moving, so heart wrenching, so beautiful and so painful at the same time, that I struggled to find a language in which to express who I was and who I had become through my journeys as a woman of the Cuban diaspora.

I began to find the language I was seeking in poetry. Although I wrote primarily in English, I would create Spanish versions of the same poems that were more often new renditions of what I was saying in English rather than literal translations. Often, snatches of a poem would come to me first in Spanish and I would move from Spanish back into English. Through this writing, I realized that my need to have a voice in the Spanish language was motivated not only by my desire to return to Cuba, but that it came as well from a yet more distant past, from my father's Sephardic ancestors who refused to stop speaking the language of those who exiled them. My poems embraced a doubled sense of loss, a language of exile that had deep roots as it sought to express the immediate and current emotional impact of being back in my childhood home as a grown woman, with a fierce longing to belong, even though I had no memories of my native land.

My return to poetry would have been impossible without the anchoring provided by my intellectual and artistic collaboration with the Cuban artist Rolando Estévez, the artistic designer of Ediciones Vigía, a publishing house founded in 1985 that produces handmade books in Matanzas, Cuba, in editions of two hundred copies. These books have become collector's items, not simply because of their small print run, but because of their excellent literary quality, their charming, whimsical designs, and the original way in which the artistry is produced on plain brown paper, proving that beautiful books can be made even within an economy and aesthetic of scarcity. Ediciones Vigía books are now known throughout the world, and major collections exist in Spain, Britain, Mexico, and the United States.

Reading and savoring the books of Ediciones Vigía opened my eyes again to the power of poetry, and of literature more generally, to speak the unspeakable, to soften our hard hearts. I was fortunate that Estévez and my friends at Ediciones Vigía encouraged my efforts at writing poetry, giving me opportunities to present my poems in Spanish to curious and compassionate audiences in Matanzas, who want to understand the desire for the island of Cubans like me, who live in the diaspora. I have had two books of poems published in Cuba by Ediciones Vigía, a small collection entitled *Poems Returned to Cuba/Poemas que vuelven a Cuba*, and recently a more ambitious collection of forty prose poems in English and Spanish entitled *Everything I Kept/Todo lo que guardé.*

Everything I Kept was inspired by and dedicated to the Cuban poet Dulce María Loynaz. The daughter of an illustrious general who fought for Cuban independence, Dulce María lived in a Havana mansion of faded elegance until her death at the age of ninety-four in 1997. Although she could have easily left Cuba after the revolution, her sense of patriotism kept her rooted on the island. Yet she wrote all of her major works before the revolution, and her wistful, meditative poems and intimate womanist fictional writing were not the kind of literature initially encouraged by the revolutionary process. She did not receive major attention for her work until advanced old age, when a younger generation of Cuban writers and artists began to seek her out as a model of artistic integrity. Later, in 1992, the Cervantes Prize was bestowed upon her by Spain, and this brought an international group of readers to her work.

It was Rolando Estévez who introduced me to the poetry of Dulce María Loynaz. When we first met, he was producing stunning watercolors in which he used fragments of her poetry in combination with artistic renderings of her work. His artistic vision drew me to the humble and yet bold quality of Dulce María's voice, the mixture of melancholy, regret, and simplicity that pervaded her writing and which has often been likened to the work of Emily Dickinson. I was especially impressed by Dulce María's volume of prose poems, *Poemas sin nombre*, published in 1953. Acclaimed at first, it was soon forgotten, even, it seemed, by Dulce María herself, who feared her work had become irrelevant in the wake of the historical transformations wrought by the Cuban revolution.

I decided to write a series of prose poems that would evoke the mood and yearning of Dulce María's poems. The majority of my

poems poured out of me in desperate haste in the last months of
my thirty-ninth year and in the first days after turning forty. I was
able to read many of these poems aloud to Dulce María, whom
I got to know, and I was especially lucky to be present at a literary event that was held in Havana in honor of her ninety-fourth
birthday, just months before her death. There is no greater gift than
being heard by a poet you love, a poet who has moved you to want
to be a poet.

In 2001, when Ediciones Vigía brought out *Everything I Kept*, I
was delighted by the design that Estévez used to present the poems.
On the cover of the book is a suitcase made out of cardboard. Inside the suitcase, which can be opened and closed with little strips
of velcro (that had to be brought to Cuba by me from the United
States, since velcro isn't available in Cuba), there are pictures of
Dulce María and me, as well as an ocean scene, complete with
sand from Varadero Beach, the famous *playa* of Cuba, where my
parents honeymooned and where I was conceived. Also inside the
suitcase is a Jewish star, wrapped in aluminum foil, marking the
fact of a Jewish presence in Cuba. The suitcase evokes the desire
to take things on one's journeys. It evokes the displacement of the
immigrant, the traveler, the anthropologist. It is also the suitcase of
our memories and dreams. And the suitcase that brims with our
ambivalent desire to keep things, to want to keep things, the desire
to keep things that shouldn't be kept, that cannot be kept.

The poems in *Everything I Kept*, a selection of which are included with these remarks, explore a variety of desires and regrets,
fears and longings. Cuba is present in the poems, but so too is the
US. The poems speak in the voice of a woman who is still searching
for home, a woman who forgets to water her garden, a woman who
longs for mangoes and has all the apples that are desired in Cuba,
a woman who is driven to desperation every winter, a woman who

has tomorrow and tomorrow. A woman for whom poetry is a cruel beast, the beast she cannot live without.

GARDEN

I passed a garden yesterday. It was planted with every kind of flower. It was flourishing, every leaf joyously green, every flower open to the light. I slowed down to look. And I remembered that my own garden had gone dry because I forgot to water it. At the beginning of spring I planted sunflowers and geraniums. When they wilted, I stopped looking at them.

That is how I have lived my life: I refuse to see the things I abandoned, the things I let die.

JARDÍN

Ayer pasé por un jardín plantado con toda clase de flores. Florecía ese jardín, cada hoja alegremente verde, cada flor abierta a la luz. Me detuve a mirar. Y recordé que mi jardín se había secado porque olvidé regarlo. Al comienzo de la primavera planté girasoles y geranios. Cuando se marchitaron, no los miré más.

Así he vivido mi vida: me niego a ver las cosas que abandoné, las cosas que dejé morir.

OBEDIENT STUDENT

I was such an obedient student that when my teachers told me I wouldn't make a good poet, I stopped writing. I adored words more than anything else in the world and preferred to cut out my tongue rather than to insult the Muses with my sickly and impoverished language. That is why these poems are so timid: like the invalid who rises from her bed after a long convalescence and walks embracing the unnatural walls.

ALUMNA OBEDIENTE

Fui una alumna tan obediente que cuando mis profesores me dije-
ron que no llegaría a ser una buena poeta, dejé de escribir. Adoraba
las palabras más que cualquier otra cosa en el mundo y preferí cor-
tarme la lengua que insultar a las Musas con mi lenguaje enfermizo
y empobrecido. Es por eso que estos poemas son tan tímidos: como la
inválida que se levanta de su cama después de una larga convales-
cencia y camina abrazándose a las paredes.

FEARS

I have so many fears: of the night, of growing old, of seeing those I
have loved fall ill or die, of my own death. Those are normal fears,
of course. But I also have stranger fears: of my heart pounding
too quickly; of unexpectedly going blind and not finding my way
home; of losing my memory before I find the time to write the
stories still dormant in me; of cold winters which will never end.
I am also afraid to get wet in the rain, to stand on my head, to run
down staircases. And police, soldiers, and immigration officers
terrify me. Yes, I am full of fears. If you took them away, I would be
weightless and free. You would see me dance like a dry brown leaf
and then I'd blow away in the autumn wind.

MIEDOS

Tengo tantos miedos: de la noche, de envejecer, de ver a los que he
querido enfermarse o morir, de mi propia muerte. Ésos son miedos
normales, por supuesto. Pero tengo miedos más raros: de que mi
corazón se ponga a latir demasiado rápido; de volverme ciega de
repente y no poder llegar a casa; de perder mi memoria antes de que
yo encuentre el tiempo de escribir los cuentos dormidos dentro de
mí; de inviernos fríos que jamás terminan. También tengo miedo a
mojarme en la lluvia, a pararme de cabeza, a bajar las escaleras de

prisa. Y los policías, los soldados, y los oficiales de inmigración me espantan. Sí, estoy repleta de miedos. Si me los quitaran, no pesaría nada y sería libre. Me verías bailar como una hoja parda, seca, y después me soplaría el viento del otoño.

FOOTPRINTS

Oh dear grandfather in your grave, remember when my beloved boy was born? You came for the circumcision in joy that your first granddaughter had the good sense to produce a son. I was happy you were happy. My love for you was primitive, unable to doubt, earnest as the last leaf on a late November maple. The wounds of my labor healed as you tucked tired geraniums into cold beds of Michigan soil. Even the muddy footprints you left on the new baby blue bathroom rug seemed odes to life, sweet reproaches to time, smears of eternity.

HUELLAS

Ay querido abuelo en tu tumba, ¿te acuerdas de cuando nació mi hermoso niño? Viniste a la circuncisión contento porque tu primera nieta tuvo la inteligencia de producir un hijo varón. Yo estaba alegre porque tú estabas alegre. Mi amor por ti era primitivo, incapaz de dudas, honesto como la última hoja de un arce a finales de noviembre. Las heridas de mi parto sanaron mientras tú acunabas mis geranios cansados en sus camas frías de la tierra de Michigan. Hasta las huellas de fango que dejaste en la nueva alfombra azulita del baño parecían odas a la vida, un reproche dulce al tiempo, manchas de eternidad.

PRAYER

This happens to me often, too often: I am on my way home, driving down familiar streets, only a few blocks to go, and out of nowhere a merciless hand comes and grips my heart and wrings it dry. I tremble. Fog clouds my eyes. I am no longer sure if I am awake or dreaming. If I die, who will find me? All I can do is pray: Let me return home, I am almost there, please . . .

I don't know why this happens. What I know is that, so far, my prayers have been answered. Hardly breathing, I reach my house. And when I open the door, I hear many keys clanging, the keys my ancestors stubbornly took with them to their exile.

REZO

Esto me pasa con frecuencia, con demasiado frecuencia: Voy camino a casa, manejando por calles conocidas, faltan solamente unas cuantas cuadras, y de no sé dónde viene una mano despiadada y agarra mi corazón y lo exprime hasta dejarlo seco. Tiemblo. Una neblina tapa mis ojos. No puedo saber ya si estoy despierta o soñando. Si me muero, ¿quién me encontrará? Lo único que puedo hacer es rezar: Déjame volver a casa, ya casi llego, por favor . . .

No sé por qué me pasa esto. Lo que sé es que, por ahora, mis rezos han sido contestados. Dejando casi de respirar, llego a mi casa. Al abrir la puerta, oigo el ruido de tantas llaves, las llaves que mis antepasados neciamente llevaron con ellos a su exilio.

LETTER

My dear friend:

I have the autumn leaves. You have the blue ocean.

I have the wide and terrifying highways of the world. You have the crumbling streets of our tearful island.

I have the fear of a lamb in a den of wolves. You have the courage of a samurai warrior.

I have silver and steel; I have a house too big for me and a calendar marking the days when I will be away; I have tomorrow and tomorrow; I have everything.

You have the witness of your eyes.

CARTA

Mi querida amiga:

Yo tengo las hojas del otoño. Tú tienes el azul del mar.
Yo tengo las carreteras anchas y espantosas del mundo. Tú tienes
las calles derrumbadas de nuestra isla llorona.
Yo tengo el miedo de un cordero en una madriguera de lobos. Tú
tienes el valor de un guerrero samurai.

Yo tengo la plata y el acero; tengo una casa demasiado grande
para mí y un calendario donde están marcados los días que no es-
taré; tengo mañana y mañana; lo tengo todo.

Tú tienes la mirada de tus ojos.

ORCHID

I bought an orchid last winter. It had a blooming flower that lasted for many months. I loved the orchid but I also loved the hand-painted ceramic pot it came in. One day the stem of the flower broke. I mourned the loss of that flower. Every morning I had held it with my eyes as I sat writing at my desk.

I missed the flower, but I knew very well that I was happy the pot was intact.

That is how I am: I cannot stand to see a beautiful ceramic pot shatter in pieces. I would rather every flower in my house wither than for one of my pots to break.

Unfortunately what you say about me is true: I seem to be more in love with things than with life itself.

ORQUIDEA

Este invierno pasado compré una orquídea. Tenía una flor que duró
muchos meses. Adoraba la orquídea pero también adoraba su mace-
ta de cerámica pintada a mano. Un día el tallo de la flor se rompió.
Lamenté la pérdida de esa flor. Todas las mañanas la había aguan-
tado con mis ojos mientras escribía en mi buró.

Extrañaba la flor, pero sabía muy bien que me alegraba de que la maceta estaba intacta.

Así soy yo: no soporto ver una linda maceta de cerámica hacerse pedazos. Prefiero que todas las flores en mi casa se marchiten a que una sóla de mis macetas se rompa.

Desgraciadamente lo que dices de mí es cierto: parece que amo más a las cosas que a la vida misma.

APPLES

I regret many things, but none so much as the time I refused to buy the five red apples for little Amanda in Cuba. The apples were very expensive, it is true. Terribly expensive, even though they had a few bruises. They were for sale in dollars and only I could buy them for her. I thought: Why does she want apples when it is the mango season and everywhere there are plump, juicy, big, yellow mangos falling from the trees? But she wanted apples, the ordinary fruit of cold northern lands. And I would not buy them for her.

Now it is autumn here and apples are everywhere. But I long for mangos.

How sour are the apples that would have made little Amanda so happy.

MANZANAS

Arrepentida estoy de muchas cosas, pero de ninguna tanto como de aquella vez que me negué a comprarle en Cuba las cinco manzanas rojas a Amandita. Las manzanas eran muy caras, es cierto. Terriblemente caras, a pesar de estar un poco estropeadas. Estaban a la venta en dólares y sólo yo podía comprarlas. Pensé: ¿Por qué quiere manzanas cuando es la época del mango y en todas partes hay gordos, jugosos, grandes, amarillos mangos cayéndose de las matas? Pero ella quería manzanas, la fruta ordinaria de las tierras frías del norte. Y yo no las quise comprar.

*Ahora estamos en otoño y hay manzanas por todas partes. Pero
yo añoro los mangos.*
*Qué agrias son las manzanas que le hubieran hecho a Amandita
tan felíz.*

BEAST
I scratch at the silence with my nails.
Look at my fingers bleed!
Poetry—cruel beast, why do you hide the words from me?

BESTIA
Con las uñas araño el silencio.
¡Mira mis dedos como sangran!
Poesía—bestia cruel, ¿por qué escondes las palabras?

OFFERING
A few months ago I would have said goodbye.
I tell you, I was ready to shut the door and not look back.
I tell you, I did not expect to touch you again.
I tell you, I had forgotten how to kiss you.
That was in winter, and winter drives me to desperation. Closed
windows, locked doors, days like shadows, and memories of an is-
land to which I will never return.
Forgive me, I lost a country, I cannot be trusted. So take this
offering. Light me like incense. Watch me go up in flames.
Turn me to ash.

OFRENDA
Hace unos meses por poco te abandono.
Te digo que ya iba a cerrar la puerta sin mirar para atrás.
Te digo que no pensaba tocarte otra vez.
Te digo que me había olvidado como besarte.

Eso fue en el invierno, y en el invierno me desespero. Ventanas cerradas, puertas bajo llave, días como sombras, y recuerdos de una isla a la que nunca voy a volver.

Perdóname, perdí un país, en mí no se puede confiar. Así que toma esta ofrenda. Préndeme como incienso. Mírame arder.

Hacerme ceniza.

6

THE DREAM
OF *NUNCA MÁS*

Healing the Wounds

– Emma Sepúlveda –

I BECAME FULLY AWARE of Vietnam in the 1960s, in South America, when I discovered the reality of an unknown war in a distant, S-shaped country of East Asia. Vietnam was conceived in my imagination through the black-and-white television screen that brought the wounded, bleeding country into the living room of my home in Chile. The impressions engraved on my memory were of a country with an open wound that bled from north to south, never healed, and only became deeper with the passage of time. In the villages and the jungle of Vietnam, from the mountains to the sea, the wound oozed with the voices, tears, screams, prayers, and pleas of mothers and children, fathers and grandparents who sought after a peace that concealed itself in the night.

Soon thereafter, I marched in street demonstrations, together with my university peers, demanding that the war on the other side of the earth end and that the spilling of more innocent blood be avoided. We were young, idealistic, and innocent. We didn't understand war, but we did understand peace. We knew that anywhere on earth, peace was better than war.

The Vietnam War stretched on for several more years. During that time, United States intervention also found its way to my country, where it quickly eradicated democracy, and surprised us by supporting the oppressive Chilean dictatorship for seventeen long years. It was then that a war that once seemed so distant and absent from our world was suddenly close to our conscience and our country. It invaded our streets, our schools, and our daily life. The history of carnage in Vietnam—which had begun to grow like an infection that spread and circulated through the veins of the world, leaving indelible imprints on everyone's memory—also left imprints in Chile. While many Vietnamese and Americans were dying in Vietnam, bodies were also being buried in Chile. People disappeared and were tortured, and those who attempted to defend human rights were terrorized.

After September 1973, we young Chileans who had protested the Vietnam War found ourselves face to face with our own war, face to face with the solitude of our own dead. The photos we had seen in the newspapers, the images of a distant and incomprehensible war in East Asia that visited us night after night on our TV screens had arrived at our own doorstep, South America. The violence of war had reached our own reality, our own country. The images were now of Chile. The bodies, the deaths, and the bullets were felt and were seen on the corners of our own neighborhoods, on the rainy forest roads of the south and the barren deserts of the north. In 1973 documents were signed that marked the beginning of the end of the war in Vietnam. But for my people, 1973 was the beginning of a dictatorship that lasted seventeen years. These two memories have remained suspended in my past.

For these reasons, the Vietnam War has endured in my memory as clearly as the remembrance of the death of democracy in

Chile. We carry these memories as if packed in a suitcase on our journey through life. Although we may wish to, we are unable to leave this burden behind at a train station or in the lonely port of a foreign country. Over the years I have opened that suitcase repeatedly and I have visited places that have inhabited my memory for decades. One of those paths, along with the many questions that had remained unanswered in my imagination since the 1970s, led me for the first time to Vietnam in 2001.

Ironically, when I returned from my trip to Vietnam, my memory was awakened again with another Tuesday, September 11 tragedy. In Chile, exactly twenty-eight years before September 11, 2001, planes soared through the blue skies above my city and dropped bombs on that spring day. The planes flew over Santiago as children were going to school, as workers commuted to factories, and as the city was awakening to the bustling of cars, buses, and pedestrians making their way from one extreme to the other of the huge metropolis. The planes flew with the purpose of destroying buildings, snuffing out lives, and taking innocent people by surprise as they awoke that sunny spring morning. The bombs fell, and following the screams and mass panic the entire city was engulfed in an overwhelming silence that spread through the streets, plazas, schools, churches, parks, and playgrounds. No one made a sound. People were incapable of even the slightest utterance. The only sensation was the sound of guns being fired and the blaring of sirens, which would never again be silenced. The explosion caused a thick black cloud to form, which rose into the sky like an immense towering wall that separated, from that day until seventeen years later, the innocent from the perpetrators. The sirens could be heard through the smoke, the cries, and the gunfire. The noise spread through time and, like the pendulum of a clock, it marked each long minute of the morning as it turned desperately into a devastating afternoon. Marching cruelly, as if on the heels of the soldiers, came that first agonizing, painful, panic-stricken night; a night that no one has ever been able to forget. That September 11 the blood-red sun hid behind the Andes mountain range. That was the day democracy died in Chile.

The violence in Vietnam, like the violence in Chile, exists now only in memory. My visit to Vietnam made me realize that although we are no longer what we were then, we still hold the reflection of the past in ourselves. Life and time have traveled along the roads, down the rivers, across rice paddies, and through the spirit of the people of Vietnam. The memory of the past survives in every niche of that land. The fruit of memory has planted the seeds of hope and has taught the lesson of beginning to forgive without forgetting. In my travels to Vietnam I wanted to draw nearer to that individual, collective, and universal memory of which we are all participants and witnesses, guilty and innocent, perpetrators and victims. And because writing has always helped to heal the wounds of my memory, I returned from Vietnam with a collection of poems, just as decades before I had come from Chile, also with poems in my suitcase.

1.
¿De dónde es Ud?
me preguntó la anciana
en Hanoi

la respuesta
nos quedó doliendo
en los dos extremos
de la memoria.

Where are you from?
the old woman in Hanoi
asked me

the answer
cut deep
into the two extremes
of our memory.

2.
La mirada de un niño pregunta:

¿Por qué piernas sin pie?
¿Por qué hombres sin brazos?
¿Por qué tantos cuerpos perdidos
en las calles del Hue?

nadie contesta sus ojos
y las conciencias se alejan
buscando refugio
en el silencio de la memoria de Vietnam
y en el mudo reflejo de nuestra propia muralla
en Washington, DC.

A child's gaze asks:

Why legs with no feet?
Why men with no arms?
Why so many lost bodies
along the streets of Hue?

no one answers his eyes
and consciences flee
searching for refuge
in the silent memory of Vietnam
and in the muted reflection of our own wall
in Washington, DC.

3.

Cruzo el puente
sobre el río Ben Hai
en la mitad del año 2002
por la ventana y tus ojos
adivino marcas secretas
de balas que cortaron
a fuego negro
el cuerpo invencible
de Hien Luong
el puente que une
el pasado y el presente
del norte y el sur

cruzo en la oscuridad
de la noche de otro siglo
el mismo puente que cruzaron
miles de vidas antes que tú y yo

voy escuchando el peso
de tus historias
en los rieles del tren

una línea tu memoria
otra línea mi memoria
sigue el tren por los rieles

una línea tu memoria
otra línea mi memoria
sigue el tren
sigue el tren

memoria interminable
por los rieles del tren
por el norte
hacia el sur
sigue el tren
sigue el tren
por todas las memorias
que cruzaron el puente
entre tu pasado y mi presente
esta noche
sigue el tren.

I cross the bridge
over the Ben Hai River
halfway into the year 2002
through the window and in your eyes
I sense the secret scars
of bullets that cut
in a hail of black fire
the invincible body
of Hien Luong
the bridge that joins
past and present
north and south

In the darkness of night
in another century
I cross the same bridge traversed
by thousands of lives
before there was a you and I

I listen to the weight
of your stories
on the train tracks

one rail your memory
another rail my memory
the train rattles along the track

one rail your memory
one rail my memory
the train rattles on
the train rattles on

unending memory
along the tracks
through the north,
heading south
the train rattles on
the train rattles on
through all the memories
that crossed the bridge
between your past and my present
tonight
the train rattles on.

The Vietnam War is now a chapter in history books. So it is
with the coup d'état in Chile. But because of Vietnam and because
of Chile, many deaths, disappearances, exiles, departures, and impossible returns are permanent images in our collective memory.
And we are all left with the task of healing the wounds that cut
deep into our memories, with nothing more than our writings and
the dream of *Never Again (Nunca Más)*.

PART TWO

THE POLITICS
OF LANGUAGE
AND IDENTITY

7

SPEAKING IN TONGUES
A Letter to Third World Women Writers

– Gloria Anzaldúa –

21 MAYO 80

Dear *mujeres de color*, companions in writing—

I sit here naked in the sun, typewriter against my knee, trying to visualize you. Black woman huddles over a desk in the fifth floor of some New York tenement. Sitting on a porch in south Texas, a Chicana fanning away mosquitos and the hot air, trying to arouse the smoldering embers of writing. Indian woman walking to school or work lamenting the lack of time to weave writing into your life. Asian American, lesbian, single mother, tugged in all directions by children, lover or ex-husband, and the writing.

It is not easy writing this letter. It began as a poem, a long poem. I tried to turn it into an essay but the result was wooden, cold. I have not yet unlearned the esoteric bullshit and pseudo-intellectualizing that school brainwashed into my writing. How to begin again. How to approximate the intimacy and immediacy I want. What form? A letter, of course.

My dear *hermanas*, the dangers we face as women writers of color are not the same as those of white women though we have many in common. We don't have as much to lose—we never had any privileges. I wanted to call the dangers "obstacles" but that would be a kind of lying. We can't *transcend* the dangers, can't rise above them. We must go through them and hope we won't have to repeat the performance.

Unlikely to be friends of people in high literary places, the beginning woman of color is invisible both in the white male mainstream world and in the white women's feminist world, though in the latter this is gradually changing. The *lesbian* of color is not only invisible, she doesn't even exist. Our speech, too, is inaudible. We speak in tongues like the outcast and the insane. Because white eyes do not want to know us, they do not bother to learn our language, the language which reflects us, our culture, our spirit. The schools we attended or didn't attend did not give us the skills for writing nor the confidence that we were correct in using our class and ethnic languages. I, for one, became adept at, and majored in English to spite, to show up, the arrogant racist teachers who thought all Chicano children were dumb and dirty. And Spanish was not taught in grade school. And Spanish was not required in high school. And though now I write my poems in Spanish as well as English I feel the rip-off of my native tongue.

I *lack imagination* you say.
No. I lack language.
The language to clarify
my resistance to the literate.
Words are a war to me.
They threaten my family.
To gain the word
to describe the loss
I risk losing everything.
I may create a monster
the word's length and body

swelling up colorful and thrilling
looming over my *mother*, characterized.
Her voice in the distance
unintelligible illiterate.
These are the monster's words.

—Cherríe Moraga[1]

Who gave us permission to perform the act of writing? Why does writing seem so unnatural for me? I'll do anything to postpone it—empty the trash, answer the telephone. The voice recurs in me: *Who am I, a poor Chicanita from the sticks*, to think I could write? How dare I even consider become a writer as I stooped over the tomato fields bending, bending under the hot sun, hands broadened and callused, not fit to hold the quill, numbed into an animal stupor by the heat. How hard it is for us to *think* we can choose to become writers, much less *feel* and *believe* that we can. What have we to contribute, to give?

Our own expectations condition us. Does not our class, our culture as well as the white man tell us writing is not for women such as us? The white man speaks: *Perhaps if you scrape the dark off of your face. Maybe if you bleach your bones. Stop speaking in tongues, stop writing left-handed. Don't cultivate your colored skins nor tongues of fire if you want to make it in a right-handed world.*

"Man, like all the other animals, fears and is repelled by that which he does not understand, and mere difference is apt to connote something malign."

—Zora Neale Hurston[2]

I think, yes, perhaps if we go to the university. Perhaps if we become male-women or as middleclass as we can. Perhaps if we give up loving women, we will be worthy of having something to say worth saying. They convince us that we must cultivate art for art's sake. Bow down to the sacred bull, form. Put frames and meta-frames around the writing. Achieve distance in order to win the coveted title "literary writer" or "professional writer." Above all do not be simple, direct, nor immediate. Why do they fight us? Because they think we are dangerous beasts? Why *are* we dangerous beasts? Because we shake and often break the white's comfortable stereotypic images they have of us: the Black domestic, the lumbering nanny with twelve babies sucking her tits, the slant-eyed Chinese with her expert hand—"They know how to treat a man in bed," the flat-faced Chicana or Indian, passively lying on her back, being fucked by the Man *a la* La Chingada.

The Third World woman revolts: *We revoke, we erase your white male imprint. When you come knocking on our doors with your rubber stamps to brand our faces with DUMB, HYSTERICAL, PASSIVE PUTA, PERVERT, when you come with your branding irons to burn MY PROPERTY on our buttocks, we will vomit the guilt, self-denial and race-hatred you have force-fed into us right back into your mouth. We are done being cushions for your projected fears. We are tired of being your sacrificial lambs and scapegoats.*

I can write this and yet I realize that many of us women of color who have strung degrees, credentials, and published books around our necks like pearls that we hang onto for dear life are in danger of contributing to the invisibility of our sister-writers. "La Vendida," the sell-out. *The danger of selling out one's own ideologies.* For the Third World woman, who has, at best, one foot in the feminist literary world, the temptation is great to adopt the current feeling-fads and theory fads, the latest half truths in political thought, the half-digested new age psychological axioms that are preached by the white feminist establishment. Its followers are notorious for "adopting" women of color as their "cause" while still expecting us to adapt to *their* expectations and *their* language. How dare we get out of our colored faces. How dare we reveal the human flesh underneath and bleed red blood like the white folks. It takes tremendous energy and courage not to acquiesce, not to capitulate to a definition of feminism that still renders most of us invisible.

Even as I write this I am disturbed that I am the only Third World woman writer in this handbook. Over and over I have found myself to be the only Third World woman at readings, workshops, and meetings. *We cannot allow ourselves to be tokenized. We must make our own writing and that of Third World women the first priority.* We cannot educate white women and take them by the hand. Most of us are willing to help but we can't do the white woman's homework for her. That's an energy drain. More times than she cares to remember, Nellie Wong, Asian American feminist writer, has been called by white women wanting a list of Asian American women who can give readings or workshops. We are in danger of being reduced to purveyors of resource lists.

Coming face to face with one's limitations. There are only so many things I can do in one day.

Luisah Teish, addressing a group of predominantly white feminist writers, had this to say of Third World women's experience:

"If you are not caught in the maze that (we) are in, it's very difficult to explain to you the hours in the day we do not have. And the hours that we do not have are hours that are translated into survival skills and money. And when one of those hours is taken away it means an hour not that we don't have to lie back and stare at the ceiling or an hour that we don't have to talk to a friend. For me it's a loaf of bread."[3]

Understand.
My family is poor.
Poor.
I can't afford a new ribbon.

The risk of this one is enough
to keep me moving through it, accountable.
The repetition like my mother's stories retold,
each time reveals more particulars gains more familiarity.
You can't get me in your car so fast.

—Cherríe Moraga[4]

"Complacency is a far more dangerous attitude than outrage."
—Naomi Littlebear[5]

Why am I compelled to write? Because the writing saves me from this complacency I fear. Because I have no choice. Because I must keep the spirit of my revolt and myself alive. Because the world I create in the writing compensates for what the real world does not give me. By writing I put order in the world, give it a handle so I can grasp it. I write because life does not appease my appetites and hunger. I write to record what others erase when I speak, to rewrite the stories others have miswritten about me, about you. To become more intimate with myself and you. To discover myself, to preserve myself, to make myself, to achieve autonomy. To dispel the myths that I am a mad prophet or a poor suffering soul. To convince myself that I am worthy and that what I have to say is not a pile of shit. To show that I *can* and that I *will* write, never mind their admonitions to the contrary. And I will write about the unmentionables, never mind the outraged gasp of the censor and the audience. Finally, I write because I'm scared of writing but I'm more scared of not writing.

Why should I try to justify why I write? Do I need to justify being Chicana, being woman? You might as well ask me to try to justify why I'm alive.

The act of writing is the act of making soul, alchemy. It is the quest for the self, for the center of the self, which we women of color have come to think as "other"—the dark, the feminine. Didn't we start writing to reconcile this other within us? We knew we were different, set apart, exiled from what is considered "normal," white-right. And as we internalized this exile, we came to see the alien within us and too often, as a result, we split apart from ourselves and each other. Forever after we have been in search of that self, that "other" and each other. And we return, in widening spirals and never to the same childhood place where it happened, first in our families, with our mothers, with our fathers. The writing is a tool for piercing that mystery but it also shields us, gives a margin of distance, helps us survive. And those that don't survive? The waste of ourselves: so much meat thrown at the feet of madness or fate or the state.

24 MAYO 80

It is dark and damp and has been raining all day. I love days like this. As I lie in bed I am able to delve inward. Perhaps today I will write from that deep core. As I grope for words and a voice to speak of writing, I stare at my brown hand clenching the pen and think of you thousands of miles away clutching your pen. You are not alone.

Pen, I feel right at home in your ink doing a pirouette, stirring the cobwebs, leaving my signature on the window panes. Pen, how could I ever have feared you. You're quite house-broken but it's your wildness I am in love with. I'll have to get rid of you when you start being predictable, when you stop chasing dustdevils. The more you outwit me the more I love you. It's when I'm tired or have had too much caffeine or wine that you get past my defenses and you say more than what I had intended. You surprise me, shock me into knowing some part of me I'd kept secret even from myself.

—Journal entry

In the kitchen Maria and Cherríe's voices falling on these pages. I can see Cherríe going about in her terry cloth wrap, barefoot washing the dishes, shaking out the tablecloth, vacuuming. Deriving a certain pleasure watching her perform those simple tasks, I am thinking *they lied, there is no separation between life and writing.* The danger in writing is not fusing our personal experience and worldview with the social reality we live in, with our inner life, our history, our economics, and our vision. What validates us as human beings validates us as writers. What matters to us is the relationships that are important to us whether with our self or others. We must use what is important to us to get to the writing. *No topic is too trivial.* The danger is in being too universal and humanitarian and invoking the eternal to the sacrifice of the particular and the feminine and the specific historical moment.

The problem is to focus, to concentrate. The body distracts, sabotages with a hundred ruses, a cup of coffee, pencils to sharpen. The solution is to anchor the body to a cigarette or some other ritual. And who has time or energy to write after nurturing husband or lover, children, and often an outside job? The problems seem insurmountable and they are, but they cease being insurmountable once we make up our mind that whether married or childrened or working outside jobs we are going to make time for the writing.

Forget the room of one's own—write in the kitchen, lock yourself up in the bathroom. Write on the bus or the welfare line, on the job or during meals, between sleeping or waking. I write while sitting on the john. No long stretches at the typewriter unless you're wealthy or have a patron—you may not even own a typewriter. While you wash the floor or clothes listen to the words chanting in your body. When you're depressed, angry, hurt, when compassion and love possess you. When you cannot help but write.

Distractions all—that I spring on myself when I'm so deep into the writing when I'm almost at that place, that dark cellar where some "thing" is liable to jump up and pounce on me. The ways I subvert the writing are many. The way I don't tap the well nor learn how to make the windmill turn. Eating is my main distraction. Getting up to eat an apple danish. That I've been off sugar for three years is not a deterrent nor that I have to put on a coat, find the keys and go out into the San Francisco fog to get it. Getting up to light incense, to put a record on, to go for a walk—anything just to put off the writing. Returning after I've stuffed myself. Writing paragraphs on pieces of paper, adding to the puzzle on the floor, to the confusion on my desk making completion far away and perfection impossible.

26 MAYO 80

Dear mujeres de color, I feel heavy and tired and there is a buzz in my head—too many beers last night. But I must finish this letter. My bribe: to take myself out to pizza. So I cut and paste and line the floor with my bits of paper. My life strewn on the floor in bits and pieces and I try to make some order out of it, working against time, psyching myself up with decaffeinated coffee, trying to fill in the gaps.

Leslie, my housemate, comes in, gets on hands and knees to read my fragments on the floor and says, "It's good, Gloria." And I think: *I don't have to go back to Texas, to my family of land, mesquites, cactus, rattlesnakes, and roadrunners. My family, this community of writers. How could I have lived and survived so long without it. And I remember the isolation, re-live the pain again.*

"To assess the damage is a dangerous act," writes Cherríe Moraga.[6]

To stop there is even more dangerous.

It's too easy, blaming it all on the white man or white feminists or society or on our parents. What we say and what we do ultimately comes back to us, so let us own our responsibility, place it in our own hands and carry it with dignity and strength. No one's going to do my shitwork, I pick up after myself.

It makes perfect sense to me now how I resisted the act of writing, the commitment to writing. To write is to confront one's demons, look them in the face and live to write about them. Fear acts like a magnet; it draws the demons out of the closet and into the ink in our pens. The tiger riding our backs (writing) never lets us alone. *Why aren't you riding, writing, writing?* it asks constantly till we begin to feel we're vampires sucking the blood out of too fresh an experience; that we are sucking life's blood to feed the pen. Writing is the most daring thing I have ever done and the most dangerous. Nellie Wong calls writing "the three-eyed demon shrieking the truth."[7]

Writing is dangerous because we are afraid of what the writing reveals: the fears, the angers, the strengths of a woman under a triple or quadruple oppression. Yet in that very act lies our survival because a woman who writes has power. And a woman with power is feared.

> "What did it mean for a black woman to be an artist in our grandmother's time? It is a question with an answer cruel enough to stop the blood."
>
> —Alice Walker[8]

I have never seen so much power in the ability to move and transform others as from that of the writing of women of color. In the San Francisco area, where I now live, none can stir the audience with their craft and truthsaying as do Cherríe Moraga (Chicana), Genny Lim (Asian American), and Luisah Teish (Black). With women like these, the loneliness of writing and the sense of powerlessness can be dispelled. We can walk among each other talking of our writing, reading to each other. And more and more when I'm alone, though still in communion with each other, the writing possesses me and propels me to leap into a timeless, space-less no-place where I forget myself and feel I am the universe. *This is power.*

It's not on paper that you create but in your innards, in the gut and out of living tissue—*organic writing* I call it. A poem works for me *not* when it says what I want it to say and *not* when it evokes what I want it to. It works when the subject I started out with meta-morphoses alchemically into a different one, one that has been dis-covered, or uncovered, by the poem. It works when it surprises me, when it says something I have repressed or pretended not to know. The meaning and worth of my writing is measured by how much I put myself on the line and how much nakedness I achieve.

> "Audre said we need to speak up. Speak loud, speak unsettling things and be dangerous and just fuck, hell, let it out and let everybody hear whether they want to or not."
>
> —Kathy Kendall[9]

I say *mujer mágica*, empty yourself. Shock yourself into new ways of perceiving the world, shock your readers into the same. Stop the chatter inside their heads. Your skin must be sensitive enough for the lightest kiss and thick enough to ward off the sneers. If you are going to spit in the eye of the world, make sure your back is to the wind. Write of what most links us with life, the sensation of the body, the images seen by the eye, the expansion of the psyche in tranquility: moments of high intensity, its move-ment, sounds, thoughts.

> "Even though we go hungry we are not impoverished of ex-periences. I think many of us have been fooled by the mass media, by society's conditioning that our lives must be lived

in great explosions, by 'falling in love,' by being 'swept off our feet,' and by the sorcery of magic genies that will fulfill our every wish, our every childhood longing. Wishes, dreams, and fantasies are important parts of our creative lives. They are the steps a writer integrates into her craft. They are the spectrum of resources to reach the truth, the heart of things, the immediacy and the impact of human conflict."

—Nellie Wong[10]

Many have a way with words. They label themselves seers but they will not see. Many have the gift of tongue but nothing to say. Do not listen to them. Many who have words and tongue have no ear, they cannot listen and they will not hear. There is no need for words to fester in our minds. They germinate in the open mouth of the barefoot child in the midst of restive crowds. They wither in ivory towers and in college classrooms.

Throw away abstraction and the academic learning, the rules, the map and compass. Feel your way without blinders. To touch more people, the personal realities and the social must be evoked— not through rhetoric but through blood and pus and sweat. *Write with your eyes like painters, with your ears like musicians, with your feet like dancers. You are the truthsayer with quill and torch. Write with your tongues of fire. Don't let the pen banish you from yourself. Don't let the ink coagulate in your pens. Don't let the censor snuff out the spark, nor the gags muffle your voice. Put your shit on the paper.*

We are not reconciled to the oppressors who whet their howl on our grief. We are not reconciled.

Find the muse within you. The voice that lies buried under you, dig it up. Do not fake it, try to sell it for a handclap or your name in print.

Love,

Gloria

NOTES

1. Cherríe Moraga, *Loving in the War Years* (Cambridge, MA: South End Press, 2000), 54–55.
2. Zora Neale Hurston, *I Love Myself When I Am Laughing: A Zora Neale Hurston Reader*, ed. Alice Walker (New York: Feminist Press, 1979), 169.
3. Luisah Teish remarks.
4. Moraga, *Loving in the War Years*, 55.
5. Naomi Littlebear, *The Dark of the Moon: Poems and Essays* (Portland, OR: Olive Press, 1977), 36.
6. Moraga, *Loving in the War Years*, 49.
7. Nellie Wong, "Flows from the Dark of Monsters and Demons: Notes on Writing," in *Radical Women Pamphlet* (San Francisco, n.p., 1979).
8. Alice Walker, "In Search of Our Mother's Gardens: The Creativity of Black Women in the South," *Ms.*, May 1974, 60.
9. Letter to author from Kathy Kendall, March 10, 1980, concerning a writers' workshop given by Audre Lorde, Adrienne Rich, and Meridel Le Sueur.
10. Wong, "Flows from the Dark of Monsters and Demons."

8

LAS AEIOUS

— Ruth Irupé Sanabria —

IT'S 1989. A fourteen-year-old Latina goes to the movies with her three homegirls. The movie is a blockbuster. They know from the commercials that it's got people who look like them in it. Who sound like them. They can't wait to see it.

They see it. They walk home. In silence. They sit on the stoop. And speak.

"Man, they can't even tell a Puerto Rican from a Mexican."

"Yeah, them accents was real fake."

"They think we's all Puerto Rican and Mexican."

"Why the Spanish girl gotta be a ho, man? I ain't a ho."

Then they fall silent again. Maybe the poem began then. Or maybe it began in 1994.

A Latina freshman is placed in the highest level Freshman Expository Writing course at a prestigious college for women. She is the only Latina in the class. This is no average expository writing class. This is a postmodern feminist theory expository writing course reserved for fifteen of the highest scoring incoming freshmen. When the Latina participates, some classmates giggle but the teacher smiles widely and makes a big show to the rest of the class of how seriously she regards her.

"You speak so cute!" a student exclaims.

They write their first paper. The professor sees the Latina after class.

"Who wrote this paper?"

"I did."

"This is not your voice. I can't accept this."

"What are you talkin' about?"

The professor explains to her what plagiarism is. The Latina retorts that she did not plagiarize.

The professor says, "I'm giving you another chance; you have until next class to turn in your paper. This time, I want to hear your voice."

The Latina walks back to her dorm. Sits on stairs. My voice? What's wrong with what I wrote?

She reads the paper aloud. Duh! It doesn't sound Barrio enough. Maybe if she throws in some "ain'ts" with a few Spanish words here and there, maybe the professor will . . .

Perhaps the poem began then.

No, it began earlier. Earlier than the movie. Earlier than grade school.

I wrote this poem for the girls on the stoops of my growing up, as an affirmation of how we speak. I mean this poem to be a defense against the racist silencing and shaming of our voices in American society today.

LAS A-E-I-O-U'S DE LOS UMS SEEKING TONGUES
OF MIGRATIN' LETRAS QUE AIN'T NO WAY HIDING

1.

gyrating spanglish verses in the rundown where dominicans loved and I watched in a city so black
they call it chocolate

is the root
word
behind this eloquence.
yo elaboraré on every detail para que usted
tenga la oportunidad to fully comprehend
the logistics of
mi latina
oral stream.

2.
The fortune tellers in the den of thieves
predict the future:
the temperature is changing
due to a warm front sweeping in from the south
south of the equator,
all of Miami and east of LA
actually, the ravage of tropical storm
TwoTongue LenguaFresca
has been taking its toll on these
southern areas
for a few centuries now
with the surfacing of a dark and mysterious dis ease.
The exotic natives of these lands were the first
to show symptoms of this
dis ease
that, according to doctors and some medicine men,
is acquired in the rare instance
that the YoNoSpeakNoInglesh Virus
comes in contact with US borders or shores.
Consequently,
these inhabitants were also the first
to show signs of immunity to this malady

as their tongues
(the area most affected by this detrimental dis ease)
developed a thick coat of repellent
resistant to psychologically induced
OneTongueAntibodies.
Though officials sought to quarantine those unfortunates
afflicted with this debilitating
enfermedad, excuse me, I mean dis ease
we now have report
that a new strain of this grave condition
has been found spreading
through most metropolitan and urbanized areas
throughout the country.
This new strain, like the previous bug,
is being attributed to the radical climatic change
triggered by a warm front sweeping in from a new southern region,
the south Bronx.
However, amid the ensuing panic,
we must remember that this dis ease
is completely preventable,
all that is required to protect you and your loved ones from catching this
dis ease
is to remain celibate from any form of unbiased cultural intercourse.
In the case that such intercourse becomes inevitable,
don't think, simply be closed minded
lack of communication is crucial, remind your infected partner that
he/she should go home, be sure to specify that you mean Mexico,
or if he/she is black you might want to suggest Puerto Rico. . . .
do not compromise your ignorance, remain firm
in forbidding the presence of any infected individual
amidst the company of you and your family,
help the community—support intolerance

donate votes to abolish bilingualism, i.e., the promiscuous abandon of
Conformity.
Spread the word
against this dis ease at your work place by promoting
mandatory acculturation and random tongue searches,
be sure to report any suspicious
dialect behavior and seize all forms of deviant rhetoric.
Promote Safe Assimilation,
with your help we can stop the spread of this dis ease.
Remember the INS is on your side.
This has been Maria Rosa Garcia Lopez
reporting en vivo, I mean quise decir
live from America.

3.
i ain't denying nothing
i'm a contradiction
in its self
an' this
is how I SPEAK so listen y escuchalo bien
cuz you know how I be feelin'
'bout repitiéndome
tú ve, es que
this is what I have become
ha ha ha
I laugh at all the
pimp mack daddy hos hooker dope crack feign perverted greasy head
mexican big tit mami rosa holy jesus jose superfly coke dealing
rapist rican mammies maids peabrained
illiterates
projected on the screen

cuz we resemble,
you know what I mean?
She always look like me
and at times,
if they did a lot of anthropological research
they even master the sound of we

4.
In college I am
an English major
thus,
fully capable of expressing
clarity of thought
in the properness of textbook
fashion, *shit*,
I mean, furthermore, I can
assess your own thoughts, so do not think too loud. . . . yes yesssss
you grapple with
spics, us Spanish folk whosho loves to talk like dat . . . ¡arriba
    arriba ándale
ándale!
But does it scare you
to know that
in the privacy
of our own homes
of our own minds
many, sp, pardon me, Latinos
you know the *good ones*
who bachelored
and mastered the white
eloquence

of *proper* English
speak this urban and rural
broke up and to'up
southern and backward
norteño and forward
speech?
and that you cant understand
or even pretend like you do?
how does it feel to be left out and out
of control?
it must feel like
time for some action
some good legal action and moral
enforcing time for some national
headbanging tongue lynching
and
none of it works
we
just
cant
seem
to get
thc fucking picture.

5.
we speak
this tree of tongued jewels
from which origins seep forth
like a brook in a forest
we gurgle the isms of recurring nightmares and
like the earth we decompose
shackles into vital minerals

listen
you will hear
staggering languages
of crossed oceans
crutched by seashells held to ears
so natural our tongues be
free of constraints
in a land where living
on earth has a fee and we are
a national nightmare realized
by the influx of aliens
encountering in-a-city realities
copulating lenguas entre labios creating
spoken masterpieces with fluid affinity
displaced immigrant words
becoming spoken refugees
as the blackboards give birth
to the ya tú sabes what's up

6.
recuerdo yo
mi primer paso
un día
a grip of years ago
en mi school
can't you see it
ooh ooh teacha look it
we took a problem and resolved it
entre los morenos
and los dominicanos
each was forced to choose
and I thought well coño fuck it

being la tremenda smartass que soy yo
I'm a let the teacher know
that I speak of where I'm from
I mirror the voices from the drone
now, she said I spoke broken
the language of the broke
the black and the foreign
so I asked her
but how bright could we be
to take two languages and make them three

7.
let me continue
que quisiera brindar
la elocuencia
de nuestra realidad
es muy simple
en su complejidad.
I scream you scream
the grandiose immigrant dream
between heaven and earth
like limbo we steam
in praise of language,
sweet words from the soul,
furiously spoken
this tongue is
as rebellious as freedom
and we speak
in slave tongues
that gum
drop stick

to the air like
the pollution
of dust
the filmy darkness
that envelops us
across the land
grammar book anarchy
is at hand.

9

ART IN AMÉRICA
CON ACENTO

– Cherríe Moraga –

I WRITE THIS ON the one-week anniversary of the death of the Nicaraguan Revolution.

We are told not to think of it as a death, but I am in mourning. It is an unmistakable feeling. A week ago, the name "Daniel" had poured from Nicaragüense lips with a warm liquid familiarity. In private, doubts gripped their bellies and those doubts they took finally to the ballot box. Doubts seeded by bullets and bread: the US-financed Contra War and the economic embargo. Once again an emerging sovereign nation is brought to its knees. A nation on the brink of declaring to the entire world that revolution is the people's choice betrays its own dead. Imperialism makes traitors of us all, makes us weak and tired and hungry.

I don't blame the people of Nicaragua. I blame the US government. I blame my complicity as a citizen in a country that, short of an invasion, stole the Nicaraguan revolution that *el pueblo* forged with their own blood and bones. After hearing the outcome of the elections, I wanted to flee the United States in shame and despair.

I am Latina, born and raised in the United States. I am a writer. What is my responsibility in this?

Days later, George Bush comes to San Francisco. He arrives at the St. Francis Hotel for a $1,000-a-plate fund-raising dinner for Pete Wilson's gubernatorial campaign. There is a protest. We, my *camarada* and I, get off the subway. I can already hear the voices chanting from a distance. We can't make out what they're saying, but they are Latinos and my heart races, seeing so many brown faces. They hold up a banner. The words are still unclear but as I come closer to the circle of my people, I am stunned. "*¡Viva la paz en Nicaragua!*" it states. "*¡Viva George Bush! ¡Viva UNO!*" And my heart drops. Across the street, the "resistance" has congregated— less organized, white, young, middle-class students. *¿Dónde 'sta mi* pueblo?

A few months earlier, I was in another country, San Cristóbal, Chiapas, México. The United States had just invaded Panamá. This time, I could stand outside the United States, read the Mexican newspapers for a perspective on the United States that was not monolithic. In the Na Bolom Center Library I wait for a tour of the grounds. The room is filled with *norteamericanos*. They are huge people, the men slouching in couches. Their thick legs spread across the floor, their women lean into them. They converse. "When we invaded Panama . . ." I grow rigid at the sound of the word, "we." They are progressives (I know this from their conversation). They oppose the invasion, but identify with the invaders.

How can I, as a Latina, identify with those who invade Latin American land? George Bush is not my leader. I did not elect him, although my tax dollars pay for the Salvadoran Army's guns. We are a living breathing contradiction, we who live *en las entrañas del monstruo*, but I refuse to be forced to identify. I am the product of invasion. My father is Anglo; my mother, Mexican. I am the result of the dissolution of bloodlines and the theft of language; and yet, I am a testimony to the failure of the United States to wholly anglicize its mestizo citizens.

I wrote in México, "*Los Estados Unidos es mi país, pero no es mi patria.*" I cannot flee the United States, my land resides beneath its borders. We stand on land that was once the country of México. And before any conquistadors staked out political boundaries, this was Indian land and in the deepest sense remains just that: a land *sin fronteras*. Chicanos with memory like our Indian counterparts recognize that we are a nation within a nation. An internal nation whose existence defies borders of language, geography, race. Chicanos are a multiracial, multilingual people, who since 1848, have been displaced from our ancestral lands or remain upon them as indentured servants to Anglo-American invaders.

Today, nearly a century and a half later, the Anglo invasion of Latin America has extended well beyond the Mexican/American border. When US capital invades a country, its military machinery is quick to follow to protect its interests. This is Panamá, Puerto Rico, Grenada, Guatemala . . . Ironically, the United States' gradual consumption of Latin America and the Caribbean is bringing the people of the Americas together. What was once largely a Chicano/Mexicano population in California is now Guatemalteco, Salvadoreño, Nicaragüense. What was largely a Puerto Rican and Dominican "Spanish Harlem" of New York is now populated with Mexicanos playing *rancheras* and drinking *cerveza*. This mass emigration is evident from throughout the Third World. Every place the United States has been involved militarily has brought its offspring, its orphans, its homeless, and its casualties to this country: Vietnam, Guatemala, Cambodia, the Philippines. . . .

Third World populations are changing the face of North America. The new face has got that delicate fold in the corner of the eye and that wide-bridged nose. The mouth speaks in double negatives and likes to eat a lot of chile. By the twenty-first century our whole concept of "America" will be dramatically altered; most significantly by a growing Latino population whose strong cultural ties, economic disenfranchisement, racial visibility, and geographical proximity to Latin America discourages any facile assimilation into Anglo-American society.

Latinos in the United States do not represent a homogenous group. Some of us are native born, whose ancestors precede not only the arrival of the Anglo-American but also of the Spaniard. Most of us are immigrants, economic refugees coming to the United States in search of work. Some of us are political refugees, fleeing death squads and imprisonment; others come fleeing revolution and the loss of wealth. Finally, some have simply landed here very tired of war. And in all cases, our children had no choice in the matter. US Latinos represent the whole spectrum of color and class and political position, including those who firmly believe they can integrate into the mainstream of North American life. The more European the heritage and the higher the class status, the more closely Latinos identify with the powers that be. They vote Republican. They stand under the US flag and applaud George Bush for bringing "peace" to Nicaragua. They hope one day he'll do the same for Cuba, so they can return to their patria and live a "North American–style" consumer life. Because they know in the United States they will never have it all, they will always remain "spics," "greasers," "beaners," and "foreigners" in Anglo-America.

As a Latina artist I can choose to contribute to the development of a docile generation of would-be Republican "Hispanics" loyal to the United States, or to the creation of a force of "disloyal" americanos who subscribe to a multicultural, mutual, radical re-structuring of América. Revolution is not only won by numbers, but by visionaries, and if artists aren't visionaries, then we have no business doing what we do.

I call myself a Chicana writer. Not a Mexican-American writer, not an Hispanic writer, not a half-breed writer. To be a Chicana is not merely to name one's racial/cultural identity, but also to name a politic, a politic that refuses assimilation into the US mainstream. It acknowledges our *mestizaje*—Indian, Spanish, and Africano. After a decade of "hispanicization" (a term superimposed upon us by Reagan-era bureaucrats), the term Chicano assumes even greater radicalism. With the misnomer "Hispanic," Anglo America proffers to the Spanish surnamed the illusion of blending into the "melting pot" like any other white immigrant group. But the Latino is neither wholly immigrant nor wholly white; and here in this country, "Indian" and "dark" don't melt. (Puerto Ricans on the East Coast have been called "Spanish" for decades and it's done little to alter their status on the streets of New York City.)

The generation of Chicano literature being read today sprang forth from a grassroots social and political movement of the sixties and seventies that was definitively anti-assimilationist. It responded to a stated mandate: *art is political*. The proliferation of *poesía*, *cuentos*, and *teatro* that grew out of El Movimiento was supported by Chicano cultural centers and publishing projects throughout the Southwest and in every major urban area where a substantial Chicano population resided. The Flor y Canto poetry festivals of the seventies and a teatro that spilled off flatbed trucks into lettuce fields in the sixties are hallmarks in the history of the Chicano cultural movement. Chicano literature was a literature in dialogue with its community. And as some of us became involved in feminist, gay, and lesbian concerns in the late seventies and early eighties, our literature was forced to expand to reflect the multifaceted nature of the Chicano experience.

The majority of published Chicano writers today are products of that era of activism, but as the Movement grew older and more established, it became neutralized by middle-aged and middle-class concerns, as well as by a growing conservative trend in government. Most of the gains made for farm workers in California were dismantled by a succession of reactionary governors and Reagan/

Bush economics. Cultural centers lost funding. Most small press Chicano publishers disappeared as suddenly as they had appeared. What was once a radical and working-class Latino student base on university campuses has become increasingly conservative. A generation of tokenistic affirmative-action policies and bourgeois flight from Central America and the Caribbean has spawned a tiny Latino elite who often turn to their racial/cultural identities not as a source of political empowerment, but of personal employment as tokens in an Anglo-dominated business world.

And the writers . . . ? Today more and more of us insist we are "American" writers (in the North American sense of the word). The body of our literary criticism grows (seemingly at a faster rate than the literature itself), we assume tenured positions in the University, secure New York publishers, and our work moves further and further away from a community-based and national political movement.

A writer will write. With or without a movement.

Fundamentally, I started writing to save my life. Yes, my own life first. I see the same impulse in my students—the dark, the queer, the mixed-blood, the violated—turning to the written page with a relentless passion, a drive to avenge their own silence, invisibility, and erasure as living, innately expressive human beings.

A writer will write with or without a movement; but at the same time, for Chicano, lesbian, gay, and feminist writers—anybody writing against the grain of Anglo misogynist culture—political movements are what have allowed our writing to surface from the secret places in our notebooks into the public sphere. In 1990, Chicanos, gay men, and women are not better off than we were in 1970. We have an ever-expanding list of physical and social diseases affecting us: AIDS, breast cancer, police brutality. Censorship is becoming increasingly institutionalized, not only through government programs, but through transnational corporate ownership of publishing houses, record companies, etc. Without a movement to foster and sustain our writing, we risk being swallowed up into the "Decade of the Hispanic" that never happened. The fact that a few of us have "made it" and are doing better than we imagined has not altered the nature of the beast. He remains blue-eyed and male and prefers profit over people.

Like most artists, we Chicano artists would like our work to be seen as "universal" in scope and meaning and reach as large an audience as possible. Ironically, the most "universal" work— writing capable of reaching the hearts of the greatest number of people—is the most culturally specific. The European-American writer understands this because it is his version of cultural specificity that is deemed "universal" by the literary establishment. In the same manner, universality in the Chicana writer requires the most Mexican and the most female images we are capable of producing. Our task is to write what no one is prepared to hear, for what has been said so far in barely a decade of consistent production is a mere *bocadito*. Chicana writers are still learning the art of transcription, but what we will be capable of producing in the decades to come, if we have the cultural/political movements to support us, could make a profound contribution to the social transformation of these Américas. The challenge, however, is to remain as culturally specific and culturally complex as possible, even in the face of mainstream seduction *to do otherwise.*

Let's not fool ourselves, the European-American middle-class writer is the cultural mirror through which the literary and theatre establishment sees itself reflected, so it will continue to reproduce itself through new generations of writers. On occasion New York publishes our work, as it perceives a growing market for the material, allowing Chicanos access to national distribution on a scale that small independent presses could never accomplish. (Every writer longs for such distribution, particularly since it more effectively reaches communities of color.) But I fear that my generation and the generation of young writers that follows will look solely to the Northeast for recognition. I fear that we may become accustomed to this very distorted reflection, and that we will find ourselves writing more and more in translation through the filter of Anglo-American censors. Wherever Chicanos may live, in the richest and most inspired junctures of our writing, our writer-souls are turned away from Washington, the US capital, and toward a México Antiguo. That is not to say that contemporary Chicano literature does not wrestle with current social concerns, but without the memory of our once-freedom, how do we imagine a future?

I still believe in a Chicano literature that is hungry for change, that has the courage to name the sources of our discontent both from within our *raza* and without, that challenges us to envision a world where poverty, crack, and pesticide poisoning are not endemic to people with dark skin or Spanish surnames. It is a literature that knows that god is neither white nor male nor reason to rape anyone. If such ideas are "naive," (as some critics would have us believe) then let us remain naive, naively and passionately committed to an art of "resistance," resistance to domination by Anglo-America, resistance to assimilation, resistance to economic and sexual exploitation. *An art that subscribes to integration into mainstream Amerika is not Chicano art.*

All writing is confession. Confession masked and revealed in the voices and faces of our characters. All is hunger. The longing to be known fully and still loved. The admission of our own inherent vulnerability, our weakness, our tenderness of skin, fragility of heart, our overwhelming desire to be relieved of the burden of ourselves in the body of another, to be forgiven of our ultimate aloneness in the mystical body of a god or the common work of a revolution. These are human considerations that the best of writers presses her finger upon. The wound ruptures and . . . heals.

One of the deepest wounds Chicanos suffer is separation from our Southern relatives. Gloria Anzaldúa calls it a "1,950-mile-long open wound," dividing México from the United States, "dividing a *pueblo*, a culture." This "llaga" ruptures over and over again in our writing, Chicanos in search of a México that never wholly embraces us. "Mexico gags," poet Lorna Dee Cervantes writes, "on this bland pocha seed." This separation was never our choice. In 1990, we witnessed a fractured and disintegrating América, where the Northern half functions as the absentee landlord of the Southern half and the economic disparity between the First and Third worlds drives a bitter wedge between a people.

I hold a vision requiring a radical transformation of consciousness in this country, that as the people-of-color population increases, we will not be just another brown faceless mass hungrily awaiting integration into white Amerika, but that we will emerge as a mass movement of people to redefine what an "American" is. Our entire concept of this nation's identity must change, possibly be obliterated. We must learn to see ourselves less as US citizens and more as members of a larger world community composed of many nations of people and no longer give credence to the geopolitical borders that have divided us, Chicano from Mexicano, Filipino-American from Pacific Islander, African-American from Haitian. Call it racial memory. Call it shared economic discrimination. Chicanos call it "Raza,"—be it Quichua, Cubano, or Colombiano—an identity that dissolves borders. As a Chicana writer that's the context in which I want to create.

I am an American writer in the original sense of the word, an Américan *con acento*.

10

THE MYTH OF THE LATIN WOMAN

– Judith Ortiz Cofer –

ON A BUS TRIP TO London from Oxford University where I was earning some graduate credits one summer, a young man, obviously fresh from a pub, spotted me and as if struck by inspiration went down on his knees in the aisle. With both hands over his heart he broke into an Irish tenor's rendition of "Maria" from *West Side Story*. My politely amused fellow passengers gave his lovely voice the round of gentle applause it deserved. Though I was not quite as amused, I managed my version of an English smile: no show of teeth, no extreme contortions of the facial muscles—I was at this time of my life practicing reserve and cool. Oh, that British control, how I coveted it. But Maria had followed me to London, reminding me of a prime fact of my life: you can leave the Island, master the English language, and travel as far as you can, but if you are a Latina, especially one like me who so obviously belongs to Rita Moreno's gene pool, the Island travels with you.

This is sometimes a very good thing—it may win you that extra minute of someone's attention. But with some people, the same things can make *you* an island—not so much a tropical paradise as an Alcatraz, a place nobody wants to visit. As a Puerto Rican girl growing up in the United States and wanting like most children to "belong," I resented the stereotype that my Hispanic appearance called forth from many people I met.

Our family lived in a large urban center in New Jersey during the sixties, where life was designed as a microcosm of my parents' casas on the island. We spoke in Spanish, we ate Puerto Rican food bought at the bodega, and we practiced strict Catholicism complete with Saturday confession and Sunday mass at a church where our parents were accommodated into a one-hour Spanish mass slot, performed by a Chinese priest trained as a missionary for Latin America.

As a girl I was kept under strict surveillance, since virtue and modesty were, by cultural equation, the same as family honor. As a teenager I was instructed on how to behave as a proper *señorita*. But it was a conflicting message girls got, since the Puerto Rican mothers also encouraged their daughters to look and act like women and to dress in clothes our Anglo friends and their mothers found too "mature" for our age. It was, and is, cultural, yet I often felt humiliated when I appeared at an American friend's party wearing a dress more suitable to a semiformal than to a playroom birthday celebration. At Puerto Rican festivities, neither the music nor the colors we wore could be too loud. I still experience a vague sense of letdown when I'm invited to a "party" and it turns out to be a marathon conversation in hushed tones rather than a fiesta with salsa, laughter, and dancing—the kind of celebration I remember from my childhood.

I remember Career Day in our high school, when teachers told us to come dressed as if for a job interview. It quickly became obvious that to the barrio girls, "dressing up" sometimes meant wearing ornate jewelry and clothing that would be more appropriate (by mainstream standards) for the company Christmas party than as daily office attire. That morning I had agonized in front of my closet, trying to figure out what a "career girl" would wear because, essentially, except for Marlo Thomas on TV, I had no models on which to base my decision. I knew how to dress for school: at the Catholic school I attended we all wore uniforms; I knew how to dress for Sunday mass, and I knew what dresses to wear for parties at my relatives' homes. Though I do not recall the precise details of my Career Day outfit, it must have been a composite of the above choices. But I remember a comment my friend (an Italian-American) made in later years that coalesced my impressions of that day. She said that at the business school she was attending the Puerto Rican girls always stood out for wearing "everything at once." She meant, of course, too much jewelry, too many accessories. On that day at school, we were simply made the negative models by the nuns who were themselves not credible fashion experts to any of us. But it was painfully obvious to me that to the others, in their tailored skirts and silk blouses, we must have seemed "hopeless" and "vulgar." Though I now know that most adolescents feel out of step much of the time, I also know that for the Puerto Rican girls of my generation that sense was intensified. The way our teachers and classmates looked at us that day in school was just a taste of the culture clash that awaited us in the real world, where prospective employers and men on the street would often misinterpret our tight skirts and jingling bracelets as a come-on.

Mixed cultural signals have perpetuated certain stereotypes— for example, that of the Hispanic woman as the "Hot Tamale" or sexual firebrand. It is a one-dimensional view that the media have found easy to promote. In their special vocabulary, advertisers have designated "sizzling" and "smoldering" as the adjectives of choice for describing not only the foods but also the women of Latin America. From conversations in my house I recall hearing about the harassment that Puerto Rican women endured in factories where the "boss men" talked to them as if sexual innuendo was all they understood and, worse, often gave them the choice of submitting to advances or being fired.

It is custom, however, not chromosomes, that leads us to choose scarlet over pale pink. As young girls, we were influenced in our decisions about clothes and colors by the women—older sisters and mothers who had grown up on a tropical island where the natural environment was a riot of primary colors, where showing your skin was one way to keep cool as well as to look sexy. Most important of all, on the island, women perhaps felt freer to dress and move more provocatively, since, in most cases, they were protected by the traditions, mores, and laws of a Spanish/Catholic system of morality and machismo whose main rule was: *You may look at my sister, but if you touch her I will kill you.* The extended family and church structure could provide a young woman with a circle of safety in her small pueblo on the island; if a man "wronged" a girl, everyone would close in to save her family honor.

This is what I have gleaned from my discussions as an adult with older Puerto Rican women. They have told me about dressing in their best party clothes on Saturday nights and going to the town's plaza to promenade with their girlfriends in front of the boys they liked. The males were thus given an opportunity to admire the women and to express their admiration in the form of *piropos*: erotically charged street poems they composed on the spot. I have been subjected to a few piropos while visiting the island, and they can be outrageous, although custom dictates that they must never cross into obscenity. This ritual, as I understand it, also entails a show of studied indifference on the woman's part; if she is "decent," she must not acknowledge the man's impassioned words. So I do understand how things can be lost in translation. When a Puerto Rican girl dressed in her idea of what is attractive meets a man from the mainstream culture who has been trained to react to certain types of clothing as a sexual signal, a clash is likely to take place. The line I first heard based on this aspect of the myth happened when the boy who took me to my first formal dance leaned over to plant a sloppy overeager kiss painfully on my mouth, and when I didn't respond with sufficient passion said in a resentful tone: "I thought you Latin girls were supposed to mature early"—my first instance of being thought of as a fruit or vegetable—I was supposed to ripen, not just grow into womanhood like other girls.

It is surprising to some of my professional friends that some people, including those who should know better, still put others "in their place." Though rarer, these incidents are still commonplace in my life. It happened to me most recently during a stay at a very classy metropolitan hotel favored by young professional couples for their weddings. Late one evening after the theater, as I walked toward my room with my new colleague (a woman with whom I was coordinating an arts program), a middle-aged man in a tuxedo, a young girl in satin and lace on his arm, stepped directly into our path. With his champagne glass extended toward me, he exclaimed, "Evita!" Our way blocked, my companion and I listened as the man half-recited, half-bellowed "Don't Cry for Me, Argentina." When he finished, the young girl said: "How about a round of applause for my daddy?" We complied, hoping this would bring the silly spectacle to a close. I was becoming aware that our little group was attracting the attention of the other guests. "Daddy" must have perceived this too, and he once more barred the way as we tried to walk past him. He began to shout-sing a ditty to the tune of "La Bamba"—except the lyrics were about a girl named Maria whose exploits all rhymed with her name and gonorrhea. The girl kept saying "Oh, Daddy" and looking at me with pleading eyes. She wanted me to laugh along with the others. My companion and I stood silently waiting for the man to end his offensive song. When he finished, I looked not at him but at his daughter. I advised her calmly never to ask her father what he had done in the army. Then I walked between them and to my room. My friend complimented me on my cool handling of the situation. I confessed to her that I really had wanted to push the jerk into the swimming pool. I knew that this same man—probably a corporate executive, well educated, even worldly by most standards—would not have been likely to regale a white woman with a dirty song in public. He would perhaps have checked his impulse by assuming that she could be somebody's wife or mother, or at least *somebody* who might take offense. But to him, I was just an Evita or a Maria: merely a character in his cartoon-populated universe.

Because of my education and my proficiency with the English language, I have acquired many mechanisms for dealing with the anger I experience. This was not true for my parents, nor is it true for the many Latin women working at menial jobs who must put up with stereotypes about our ethnic group such as: "They make good domestics." This is another facet of the myth of the Latin woman in the United States. Its origin is simple to deduce. Work as domestics, waitressing, and factory jobs are all that's available to women with little English and few skills. The myth of the Hispanic menial has been sustained by the same media phenomenon that made "Mammy" from *Gone with the Wind* America's idea of the black woman for generations; Maria, the housemaid or counter girl, is now indelibly etched into the national psyche. The big and the little screens have presented us with the picture of the funny Hispanic maid, mispronouncing words and cooking up a spicy storm in a shiny California kitchen.

This media-engendered image of the Latina in the United States has been documented by feminist Hispanic scholars, who claim that such portrayals are partially responsible for the denial of opportunities for upward mobility among Latinas in the professions. I have a Chicana friend working on a Ph.D. in philosophy at a major university. She says her doctor still shakes his head in puzzled amazement at all the "big words" she uses. Since I do not wear my diplomas around my neck for all to see, I too have on occasion been sent to that "kitchen," where some think I obviously belong.

One such incident that has stayed with me, though I recognize it as a minor offense, happened on the day of my first public poetry reading. It took place in Miami in a boat-restaurant where we were having lunch before the event. I was nervous and excited as I walked in with my notebook in my hand. An older woman motioned me to her table. Thinking (foolish me) that she wanted me to autograph a copy of my brand-new slender volume of verse, I went over. She ordered a cup of coffee from me, assuming that I was the waitress. Easy enough to mistake my poems for menus, I suppose. I know that it wasn't an intentional act of cruelty, yet of all the good things that happened that day, I remember that scene most clearly, because it reminded me of what I had to overcome before anyone would take me seriously. In retrospect I understand that my anger gave my reading fire, that I have almost always taken doubts in my abilities as a challenge—and that the result is, most times, a feeling of satisfaction at having won a convert when I see the cold, appraising eyes warm to my words, the body language change, the smile that indicates that I have opened some avenue for communication. That day I read to that woman and her lowered eyes told me that she was embarrassed at her little faux pas, and when I willed her to look up at me, it was my victory, and she graciously allowed me to punish her with my full attention. We shook hands at the end of the reading, and I never saw her again. She has probably forgotten the whole thing but maybe not.

Yet I am one of the lucky ones. My parents made it possible for me to acquire a stronger footing in the mainstream culture by giving me the chance at an education. And books and art have saved me from the harsher forms of ethnic and racial prejudice that many of my Hispanic *compañeras* have had to endure. I travel a lot around the United States, reading from my books of poetry and my novel, and the reception I most often receive is one of positive interest by people who want to know more about my culture. There are, however, thousands of Latinas without the privilege of an education or the entrée into society that I have. For them life is a struggle against the misconceptions perpetuated by the myth of the Latina as whore, domestic, or criminal. We cannot change this by legislating the way people look at us. The transformation, as I see it, has to occur at a much more individual level. My personal goal in my public life is to try to replace the old pervasive stereotypes and myths about Latinas with a much more interesting set of realities. Every time I give a reading, I hope the stories I tell, the dreams and fears I examine in my work, can achieve some universal truth which will get my audience past the particulars of my skin color, my accent, or my clothes.

I once wrote a poem in which I called us Latinas "God's brown daughters." This poem is really a prayer of sorts, offered upward, but also, through the human-to-human channel of art, outward. It is a prayer for communication, and for respect. In it, Latin women pray "in Spanish to an Anglo God / with a Jewish heritage," and they are "fervently hoping / that if not omnipotent, / at least He be bilingual."

11

THE QUINCENTENARY CONFERENCE AND THE EARTH SUMMIT, 1992

– Rigoberta Menchú –

I HAVE BEEN GOING round the world for years, to house after house, to town after town and to different countries. I have gotten lost in airports, in buses and in train stations. I have been invited to many places. People have gradually got to know me. I am like a drop of water on a rock. After drip, drip, dripping in the same place, I begin to leave a mark, and I leave my mark in many people's hearts.

Over a period of ten years, from my first visit to the United States in May 1982 until the end of 1991, I had the good fortune to meet an enormous number of people—in solidarity groups, in women's organisations, and in ethnic groups. In the early days, I was happy if there was just one photographer or journalist at my press conferences. I had no complexes. I talked about Guatemala and about indigenous peoples. I told my life story, and discussed my childhood, my youth and my first book.

I learned a lot by listening to other people. I did not learn from reading but by listening to young people's problems, marital problems, society's insensitivity and people's intolerance. I listened to the voices of other victims of oppression, and sometimes we would end up crying, not just for Guatemala, but for all the things they had gone through too.

If I talk about specific problems in other countries, it is not because I have read about them in a book, but because people have told me about them. People usually start by asking me about Guatemala. Then they compare it with their own reality, and soon they begin talking about their own uncertainties and hopes and aspirations. People cry out in pain all over the planet. All these speaking tours have come about quite spontaneously. We never had a particular itinerary. There was no decision to follow a particular line.

Somebody had to do it. If no one had done it before, it was because no one had had the opportunity. They weren't as privileged as I was. Nothing was planned. If it had been, it might not have got very far. These things are like footprints on a path, like the smell of the earth after the rain; they happen by themselves.

In 1993, we went on a tour of twenty-eight countries. It was very hard work. In each country the days were packed with arranged meetings and activities. On top of that, there were the unexpected events. We might suddenly have to go to a special function with presidents, ministers, royalty, celebrities, "important people." Even though we had had twelve years' experience of using elegant knives and forks, we still found it difficult. In contrast we might visit Burmese refugees in Thailand, or indigenous people in Santa Maria del Este in Argentina or Chimborazo in Ecuador. We might get to countries where they eat and live differently, or where we had to take our rubber shoes off and walk through the mud.

You have to be with people, live the lives they lead and feel how they feel. We might go to elegant houses and feel very tense, and have to be careful about what we did and said. From there we'd go to a world of poor marginal people. We'd feel so weary and conscience-stricken, and also so full of admiration for these people's courage. That happened everywhere we went.

Sometimes, after fifteen days with a team of workers, I felt I needed to change them so that we didn't all get tired together. I would return to Mexico, leave one team behind, and set off again with another. There was no alternative. It's been like that for the last few years.

In 1992, there were the celebrations of the Quincentenary of the Spanish "discovery" of America. I learned many things that year. It's no secret that I had many problems with the official Spanish Commission on the Quincentenary, especially the team dealing with indigenous peoples. The commission included a particular racist whose name I choose not to mention. He defended the most indefensible positions.

We had started organising a counter-campaign in 1989 when we first heard that the Spanish Commission was bent on celebrating the Quincentenary. Our people said that there wasn't anything to celebrate. On the contrary, the occasion offended us and generations of our ancestors. It was no cause for celebration, and even less a meeting of two cultures. We wanted to commemorate our ancestors, and remember them with a dignity worthy of the coming century. If the Spanish Commission thought the date was so important, they should have given us the opportunity to participate as protagonists in our own history.

In 1989, we managed to hold our first continental Quincentenary Conference in Colombia. The original idea came from the indigenous movements in Ecuador (CONAI), Colombia (ONIC), and Guatemala (CUC). The first conference, organised initially to support the landless peasants of Brazil, brought together all the active indigenous organisations in America and began the "Five Hundred Years of Resistance" campaign.

By the time of the second conference, held in Guatemala in 1991, we had included not only the Caribbean, but also popular movements throughout the continent. We changed the name of the campaign to "Five Hundred Years of Indigenous, Black, and Popular Resistance."

By 1992, we had decided to change course again, to make it a continental movement and not just a campaign. Hitherto we had followed the approach that governments were taking to the Quincentenary. Now we wanted to approach it in a different way, looking towards the year 2000. In our struggle, we always follow a star—a long-term vision—in this case, the prospect of a better life for oppressed and marginalised sectors and the achievement of full recognition for the indigenous peoples of the world.

The financial resources for organising these activities came from thousands of people: solidarity committees, women's groups, youth groups, human rights groups, small institutions in Europe and the United States. A large part came from the Evangelical churches and from the National Council of American Churches, the World Council of Churches, and the International Lutheran Federation. Collecting this money was not easy. Certain institutions put us through a kind of Spanish Inquisition first before they would part, reluctantly, with a thousand dollars or five thousand dollars—when they could have given us so much more. To powerful institutions like the Catholic Church, our activities smacked of subversion or communism. It was as if we were the Devil undermining their belief. They could never understand why our people criticised the Quincentenary. They thought we were just being aggressive, and they were suspicious of us. Yet, as always, we also found good and generous allies, and these we will not forget.

We indigenous peoples live in different parts of the American continent, we have different experiences and identities, and we also have diverse and multiple dreams. Each of us has survived alone, in our own nations, without contact with other indigenous peoples. Just as I was not aware that there were other Mayans before I went to Mexico, the indigenous peoples of Latin American have not known a great deal about each other. Yet the fundamental bases of our culture unite us, because they are ancient cultures.

We discovered that indigenous peoples have always contributed valuable things to society through their labour and culture, their art and medicine, their wisdom and patience. They have contributed their own blood and pain to build the so-called democracies, a contribution that has never been recognised. On the contrary, a good number of our mestizo children have been denied participation in our ancient culture, and have been made to feel ashamed of the earth which bore them and of their roots.

By the time of the Quincentenary in 1992, the indigenous peoples of America had begun to have a common vision, shared demands, and a sense of solidarity. The majority of our peoples have a vision. They foresee a great future. They have dreams, and the determination to see them take shape, for the sense of community is sacred, and something of real value in this day and age. We called our third conference, which took place in Nicaragua that October, "The Conference of Self-Discovery." The huge majority of our people are poor. We discovered that if poor people unite they can achieve results. Before we got funding, we had to take a few *centavos* from each family, from our children's mouths, for our projects to materialise. The expenses of our early meetings were borne by our own families. Our community is the reason why we are still alive, why we are still here five hundred years after the Conquest. We have survived amid the rubble of endless massacres. If our peoples had disintegrated, if they had lost their languages, if they had lost their communities, their collective way of life, their concept of leadership, they would have died out. We discovered that if we unite, if we recognise our organisations' leaders and avoid rivalries, we will achieve the results we seek.

We also discovered that we have not simply been spectators during these five hundred years. We have been protagonists as well. We realised how often our intellectual rights have been usurped, how our thinking has been manipulated and distorted. Since 1989, the world has rediscovered indigenous wisdom. This is a source of pride for us. I am pleased that the thoughts and lives of our peoples have become more widely known. Yet the more they are known, the more they have become a commercial product. Our profound appreciation of the relationship between Mother Nature and people's lives has been exploited over and over again, by environmentalists, writers and celebrities. Voluminous works plagiarising our thinking have appeared, apparently magical works pulled out of the air by famous brains, the sole authors of indigenous thought. They have stolen these concepts from us and not given us credit.

They don't say, "This is what the Yanomamis think, or the Mayans, or the Aztecs." Or, "This wisdom comes from the native peoples of the Pacific, or the Maoris." They don't say, "This is the wisdom of ancient cultures, therefore we respect it, we borrow it to share with other people." No, these are simply great brains who have suddenly discovered the importance of harmony.

When I read a poem about nature and find that it is actually a Hopi or Navajo saying, and that the poet does not recognise the source and presents it as his own work, it makes me very suspicious. They never say, "Chief Descage said this." Or, "A Mayan chief said this." Or, "A Chorti woman, a Chamula woman, said this." They never explain that these concepts had ancient roots. That is why people often think that indigenous peoples have no body of thought. I know that a people's experiences, values, and wisdom do not belong to any one individual and should be universal patrimony. It offends me when this patrimony is simply used to benefit certain individuals.

I don't like saying things like this, but sometimes you have to talk plainly in order to be understood and to make friends. It teaches you who your real friends are, and I want my friends to know what I think. In our culture, our word is our bond. This does not just refer to the spoken word, it also means commitment, feelings, responsibility, frankness. These are values one receives as a child, and we should reaffirm their importance. I go back to the time when I learned our culture from my elders. Yet paradoxically, to be able to talk about it, I had to physically leave my village and my wider community.

By the time of the third conference, we were delighted to see that the exchanges between our leaders had reached a qualitatively different level. Our efforts had given dignity to the human race. The Quincentenary taught me something: that the young five-hundred-year-old culture of the invader (a bloody culture with many inherent problems) had wanted to rapidly eliminate the memory of a culture that was thousands of years old. Yet five hundred years is nothing. It takes a lot longer to destroy an ancient culture.

Cultures have roots, a heart, a meaning. Hopefully, in the future, one culture will not impose itself on another in this way. Cultures will fuse, not by massacres, sterilisation, repression, and destruction, but through mutual respect.

I happened by chance to be at the Earth Summit held in Rio de Janeiro in 1992. I had been invited to Brazil by various church organizations for another conference, and I was curious to see what the Summit was like. So I paid my fifty-dollar entrance fee and went in. I couldn't get through the security barriers that prevented ordinary people from going into the official conference, so I went in what was called the "global arena." It was a very disappointing spectacle. Indigenous people were dancing for the public in a sort of folklore show. It turned out to be a load of blond people pretending to be Amazon Indians.

Some journalists came over to interview me, not because they recognised me but because I looked indigenous in my colourful costume. They asked me what I thought. I said, "It's entertaining. There's a lot to buy. I've enjoyed myself, I've watched Indians in feathers dance. I've seen lots of T-shirts, plastic bags, and postcards being sold. But I wonder how many trees were cut down to make them." I didn't tell them my name because it wasn't important.

I had gone to find out what their idea of the earth, plants, and nature might be, and what I found was a commercial version of ecology. There were T-shirts with tigers, lions, and parrots painted on them, and plastic bags with animals' faces. It was a case of businessmen making money out of the environment. They usurped indigenous wisdom and made films to sell to make even more money. They prostituted the thoughts of the indigenous peoples. I had the feeling that the organisers weren't very clear about the difference between indigenous people and wild animals, between protecting the jungle and exploiting it. A love affair with nature has its limits when it comes to making money.

Yet the Earth Summit undoubtedly did a lot of good. It made young people think about environmental issues. Intellectuals devoted a moment of their time to studying the problem, and the views of representatives of ancient cultures were listened to. It was a big success for us, it had worldwide exposure. The danger is that protecting the environment has become fashionable; it is a fad that may not last.

I walked around the streets and went into neighborhoods, and I was recognised by certain nuns and priests. We went to see what they call "street children" and people lost in the precarious life of poverty. We heard many sad stories. People said, "There used to be lots of children on the streets but they had a cleanup before the

Earth Summit." We asked what they meant by a cleanup. "Well, they rounded the kids up and took them a long way away." That's what we were told.

A great many people assured us there was a city where all the children had been taken. I would have liked to find it. In some corner of Brazil were about thirty thousand kids who had been cleared off the city streets to prepare for the Earth Summit? Did it mean they were in some center, or in a special barracks, or in a hospital, bottled up and ready to be sold? What did "taking them away" mean?

A lot of people said they had been killed. "Well, they weren't any use," they declared. "Why weren't they any use?" I asked. "Because they were layabouts, they hung around the streets, and they stole. Some were ill, and they probably weren't given medicine. They're bound to be dead."

I felt so impotent. I didn't know what to do. I felt guilty just knowing about it.

They were also holding an indigenous people's conference which if I remember rightly was called the Carioca Conference. It was being held simultaneously with the Rio Summit. It aimed to produce an indigenous model for the next decade. I was curious to see what the model was, so I went along. If our houses were like those on show, it would indeed be a gift from God. Perhaps by the end of the decade our people will live in houses like that. They had concrete foundations that made them very stable. They were well built and attractive. Their architects had studied various types of houses in Brazil and had come up with this model house, large and spacious too.

The difference between the two conferences was that the Carioca one was more authentic. Much of the folklore had been organized so that indigenous people performed for each other rather than being put on show as exotica. Even so, there were plenty of dirty blond people with long hair who were pretending to be Indians, or wanted to be indigenous, or sympathized with indigenous peoples. I came to the conclusion that we don't need handouts or charity. We just want the chance for people themselves to take the decisions that affect their future.

After that I went to an ecumenical conference. Priests from various countries, of varying origins, and with various levels of social commitment, were there. This conference raised my spirits because it dealt with problems rigorously and critically. They looked at environmental issues from a moral point of view.

I stayed on in Brazil a few more days, doing my usual lobbying: cornering people to ask to be allowed to put our case, giving my opinion on issues they were tackling, finding out whether one thing was more important than another, and generally investigating what was going on. I spent still more time consolidating ties with indigenous groups and getting in touch with peasant organisations that were possibly there for the same reasons as me, but just a bit lost.

I often ask myself what the point is of our being here, we who are part of nature too. How will we be able to buy air and water, how will we be able to live? Human beings should think more carefully about the damage they are doing to life. Brazil has a very significant role because of the immense natural wealth it has available to sell to powerful trans-national companies. How much wood did it sell despite the conference? How much bargaining went on? How many deals were signed? And how many economic and political concessions were made before they reached agreement?

I didn't get answers to a lot of questions I asked that year. There are defining moments in our lives that raise our awareness. It is a different kind of awareness from what you get from books, it comes from direct experience. I was lucky enough to have been to the Earth Summit because it made me aware that the struggle of indigenous people to protect the environment is different from the struggles of other peoples. Ours is not just a passing fancy. We protect our environment, our air and our water by the way we live. It is our very life.

The solution to our problems of poverty is not just more money. It lies in more equal distribution. It may also mean eradicating fundamental inequalities, abolishing privileges, and purging the development agencies. At the moment, we have government bodies full of experts with money in their pockets, who believe they hold the key to development. We also have poor peasants who have nothing and whose only value is as a theoretically developable object. This is a situation that has to change.

I have been very critical of the International Monetary Fund (IMF) and the World Bank. I think these organisations deal very badly with problems of human-rights violations and the environment. If they didn't deal with them so badly, the scorched-earth campaign in Guatemala could have been prevented, and new laws governing land distribution introduced. How can the World Bank allow huge areas of land to be used to pasture a few cows, so that land-owning and bourgeois families can spend their weekends killing deer? How can they allow this at a time when millions of people are starving because they have no land? How can it permit huge land concessions that destroy the natural world by trafficking in wood, rare animals and archaeological remains?

I continue to think that the IMF and the World Bank have a direct responsibility for the extreme poverty that plagues the majority of the world's population. I still hope these institutions can bring about change, not with words, but with actions. There must be forms of economic planning and concrete measures that demonstrate to poor people the good will and generosity of these institutions.

In the absence of such large institutions, indigenous people have developed a spirit of co-operativism. This has been a way of instilling collective responsibility. It is not based solely on economic progress. I defend cooperative values wholeheartedly. It is a system of organization, a way of life, a culture. Throughout the world, poor people are able to survive because they co-operate. They need to organise to combat social injustice and the unequal distribution of wealth. They need solidarity. Day after day, in their neighborhoods, villages, and municipalities, they face adversity—a brother's death, a relative's illness, a child being orphaned—in the tangible way that only the wretched of this earth really know. Charities program their aid, but poor people contribute twenty-four hours a day. Charities choose which of the poor they want to help, but poor people don't have a choice. They are born with a caring heart. It is not only indigenous people who have this sense of solidarity.

That's why I argue that the struggle of indigenous peoples has a purpose—to represent all oppressed people in the world. If we were the only ones, we might act differently, because we have been wise enough to realize what was being done to us. Yet the fact is that poverty does not only affect indigenous peoples. It affects black people, mestizos, and all the world's dispossessed. Suffering knows no frontiers.

In recent years, in their haste to control indigenous peoples and change the way they live, and perhaps to avoid internal conflicts, international agencies have tried to undermine the value of co-operatives. One of their strategies has been to create phoney NGOs. In our own experience, most of the experts in these NGOs are foreigners from the developed world. If they are not actually foreign, they tend to think and act like foreigners. They come with the idea that indigenous peoples understand nothing about development, and have no projects of their own. They believe that they have to educate them, like a species that can be trained to understand the principles of development. Their arrogance and deep paternalism so blinds them that they are unable to see the positive things and solutions that are already there. This has meant they have made many mistakes. In the end they merely create what I call "parasites on society." These are harsh words, I know. Not everyone is like this, but all suffer the same consequences.

We are talking about people who have made careers out of promising development. I had travelled all over the continent and visited most of the countries in the Americas long before I received the Nobel Prize. I know most of the local development agencies. I am not wrong when I say that these bodies undermine the people's own organisations and leaders, imposing on them groups or organisms that just serve to channel funds. A lot of money has gone to poor countries without anyone bothering to investigate properly whether it actually reaches the people. In the majority of cases, ridiculous, paternalistic, and discriminatory policies are in force. How can you explain the fact that an expert lives in an area for fifteen years and then, when he leaves the community, it is poorer than before he came? What development has he taught?

The problem usually occurs because two different languages are being used. One is the language of the expert who comes from, and thinks in terms of, the First World. He earns an absurd salary; he earns in a month what poor people earn in two years. The other is the pragmatic language of local people. As a result, oppressive situations are re-created. The problem facing these agencies in the coming years will be for them to win back the people's trust. Poor people are not for sale, our poverty is not for sale. Yet the great craving for development that has been awoken in our people still has to be satisfied.

Government agencies have to realise that our people can contribute knowledge, techniques, wisdom, and labour. We could perhaps work on projects together, ones that are more humane, sensitive, and respectful of the environment. We might have to find criteria for training experts so there might be a point at which our knowledge and that of the expert could be mutually beneficial. The development experts need our people and we need them. We could both contribute to a more secure future.

I got these ideas about the dialogue between different cultures from having stayed in the houses of many different people all round the world. I always ask a lot of questions on my solidarity tours. I have taken part in countless conferences about development and the eradication of poverty. I have spoken to audiences of hundreds of people.

These last few years have brought hundreds of new experiences. I have earned the affections of many people. I have been given flowers and wonderful hospitality. I don't have a single bad memory of any of the homes I visited, and I don't think any have bad memories of me. I tried to be respectful to all my hosts. I respected their food, their homes, their customs. I tried to learn things that were not easy for me.

It was hard for me when I discovered the consumer society, the society of waste: to see food and objects thrown away; to go to a vast supermarket and see all the food for cats and dogs, at incredible prices; to think of all the protein that this food contains, and to know that we never had food of that quality.

I also learned a lot about women and children. It was strange for me to discover about feminism and Islam, and about all the other beliefs I had not known about in the mountains of Chimel. Some of the things I discovered, I just couldn't understand. I couldn't understand how a woman could be with another woman. I had never heard of homosexuality. I was like a child who doesn't understand, who questions and asks. It was hard to understand how people complicated their lives so much. I found lesbianism very strange because it has nothing to do with the way I was brought up. Yet in the end I don't have to understand it to respect it. Respect for others is bigger than my small world. I have talked to several women friends and they have told me a lot about their lives. Theirs were very unusual circumstances. I have come to realize that each person's life comes from their own experience and is the result of their own decision.

I have a great friend who is homosexual. I met him in New York. He is openly homosexual. He is a wonderful man, very courteous and refined, and with a simplicity that shows his pureness of heart. I was always very curious, but I never enquired about the details of his life. I was naive about such matters, though I knew it was a controversial subject. I have always thought it is better to be reticent and not get involved in the whys and wherefores. I was more interested in understanding than in passing judgement. This is perhaps because we indigenous peoples have always been misunderstood, and many people think that our difference is a reason to despise us.

When we fight for our rights, we are called indigenous, but if we take our demands further than indigenous rights, then we are called communists. If we include women's rights, we are not only indigenous communists but feminists too. They put labels on us to devalue our struggle. This hurts us deeply, so our understanding of others comes from that too. We know that other underprivileged or misunderstood groups face similar problems. They are marginalized like us.

In indigenous societies, homosexuality might exist but it would probably be integrated within our society. Most of our people get married between the ages of fourteen and sixteen, and they lead a very close-knit family life. In recent years, however, some women live alone or some men don't get married. The indigenous community absorbs differences, be they sexual, mental, or physical.

Disabled people in our villages are integrated into the community, that is, they are looked after by their family who treat them as equals. Everybody treats them with respect, because disability is considered normal—because it is Nature's work too. We are taught from the time when we are very little that making fun of a disabled person brings a curse from Nature upon our heads. It is like offending something sacred.

The same goes for pregnant women. You can't eat in front of a pregnant woman without offering her some of your food. Otherwise you would hurt her feelings and those of the baby she is carrying. So disabled people and pregnant women are thought of in the same way. In this respect, I think Western society has lost its sense of balance. Human beings are different from animals, there is something more profound in them than in animals. An animal doesn't care what it does in public, whereas human beings are more discreet. Not for any moral reason but because there are sacred aspects of life which must be given total respect.

Mayan women are very hardworking. The sense of family, the feeling for life, the duality of life, is a philosophical and conceptual principle that governs their existence. Yet the position of women is very unfavorable at present. We too are fighting for better treatment and better conditions. We are fighting to achieve full and effective political participation. This doesn't mean sterilizing women so they can't have any more children. Our problem is not our children, but having access to science, technology, knowledge, development, and the legal system. We want equal opportunities, and to have them within the norms of our own culture.

As we near the end of the century, we can see all too clearly how some categories of human beings have been marginalized. An outrageous example of this is the war in the former Yugoslavia, where it was women who suffered the worst kind of violence. Throughout history women have always been raped in war. The very nature of motherhood, the very basis of femininity, has always been used as a weapon of war. What has happened as part of ethnic cleansing in the former Yugoslavia is horrifying and shameful, not only because it is a repetition of crimes committed fifty years ago under the Nazis, but because it has been happening at a time when everyone is preaching development, progress, and modernity.

I was deeply disturbed when I realized what was being done to women. Forcing a woman so that she gives birth to the fruit of an act of violence is too terrible to imagine. If we, the women of the world, were to unite and organize, we could break down the frontiers of silence with our cries of condemnation. We could raise the cause of these women as a battle cry that would live forever in our common memory as a gender, as the givers of life and creators of hope.

We must never forget these women. It is almost as if there were a curse on them. Those Muslim mothers will never be accepted by those of their religion because they have been raped by strangers. It is like a human sacrifice. The rape of a Muslim woman is like making a human sacrifice to the Gods of War, Capitalism, and Power. What hope is there for the children when they are born? It is all bound up with the distribution of wealth, individual ambition, men and women's alienation, and the abuse of military power.

How would I feel if I were a Muslim woman in that situation? How could I even bear the touch of my own skin? We have to put ourselves in their place. I am astounded that people dare tell them what to do. All those arguments we hear so much of, about whether they have the choice to abort babies conceived as a result of rape. There are world leaders who tell them that abortion is a sin. I have the deepest respect for the determination of these women, and I have to confess that I never agreed with those who begged these women not to have abortions. I respect world leaders, but this time they made my blood run cold. Their message went right against my own ethics, and my experience as a victim. If a woman has been raped, she and she alone knows what this act of cruelty means, and she alone must decide how to deal with it.

When the Spaniards arrived five hundred years ago, they raped our ancestors, our grandmothers, our mothers, to breed a race of mestizos. The result is the violence and cruelty that we are still living with today. The Spaniards used a vile method to create a mixed race, a race of children who doubted their own identity, with their heads on one side of the ocean and their feet on the other. That is what happened to our culture.

Admiring other cultures is fine, but the imposition of one culture on another is not. Mestizo society in America is not the result of a process of understanding within that society. I don't mean that the mixing of races is a bad thing; it is just that cultures must learn to live together. Intellectuals like José Carlos Mariltegui defied the rules imposed on them by a society that devalued their roots and their reality. People like these make history, because they are part of our identity as a continent. Their ideas and their struggles have transcended society. The past cannot just be about myths. It must be a source of strength for the present and the future. All the good things that have come out of our continent, even the ideas that we once regarded as superficial and useless, must be re-examined. We have to blend our two cultures, the ancient and the modern. We should not be trying to eradicate anything or anybody because we think one is better. We should be trying to find a way of living together, combining the ancient culture of our peoples with the culture of the colonizers. That is the strength of our American identity, the privilege of having roots that go back for thousands of years.

The crises that a society goes through are also part of its history. They show us the way forward, they shape our culture. You can't go back and change history, nor can you make it an excuse for not changing the future. We can make the future different, we can make it better.

Looking back, I think perhaps it was a mistake to turn the Quincentenary celebrations into a kind of battlefield. Many people want to return to the old Inca and Mayan ways of five hundred years ago. It is impossible to do that! How can we go back and be the same? Indigenous tradition itself says that time is long and wide, and it has its own signs. Each sign has a different meaning, it may mean the time has come for a generation of great leaders or great achievements. That is a sign of the time and you cannot go against it. On the other hand, it is wrong to simply praise the victors. We should accept that things can always be improved.

Many people believe that indigenous peoples have been no more than spectators over the past five hundred years, that we are the conquered people. It is true that we have been the victims of racism, discrimination, and oppression. We know exactly what colonization means. It means terrible exploitation and humiliation. But people should remember that indigenous peoples built great cities with our own hands, we created the most wonderful works of art with the sweat of our brows. All were carefully designed and built in our own distinctive way. We have contributed so much to the richness of our peoples in America that it is impossible to say where indigenous culture begins and ends.

Culture isn't pure, it is dynamic, it is a kind of dialectic, it is something that progresses and evolves. As for purity, who can determine what that means? I don't think our peoples were ever passive bystanders. The advances made have just as much been ours, for we contributed to them, just as we have contributed to the enormous ethnic diversity. I think the whole idea of purity is damaging, it leads to sectarianism, intolerance, segregation and racism.

A lot of different attitudes emerged during the Quincentenary. Some of our brothers believed that the purity of the Mayan, Inca, and Aztec cultures still exists, others proclaimed that the times favored the ancient cultures. Then there are those who believe that human destiny is intercultural, that unity lies in recognizing differences. I believe that the revival of ancient values does not benefit indigenous peoples alone.

Our *ajq'iij* had the right idea. They didn't argue over whether our ancestors were better or worse, whether one person was purer than another, whether *ladinos* were purer than us, whether *ladinos* should live like Indians. They taught us that war destroyed indigenous dignity and unity. They didn't say if you belong to our tribe you are pure, and if you don't belong, you're not. They didn't waste their time on nonsense like that. The *ajq'iij* were simple men, and wise at the same time. They said, "Now is the time for the rain to fall and make the seeds grow on our soil and make our culture flourish, so let there be no more discord." They told us when the rains would come and when there would be light, to light our path. This light would make us recognize our identity, recognize who we are, make us think in a different way. When one cycle is completed, then we are in a new cycle.

This is very closely bound up with the issue of the environment that seems to be one of the main themes in this new cycle. The most important thing about the Earth Summit in Rio de Janeiro was that it generated debate everywhere, from the indigenous communities to the most elegant salons. I attended countless women's conferences and youth conferences. Young people are beginning to care much more about the environment. People are becoming more environmentally conscious, and when there is awareness of a problem, there is positive action and solutions are found. Sometimes this sort of thing may just be a fashion, and this can prove negative. But I think the past few years have been very fruitful as far as environmental awareness is concerned.

Indigenous peoples have always cared about the environment, we learned about it from our elders. Now we can make a much bigger and better contribution. We have to say to the world, "Listen, we want to have our say, because we love Mother Earth and we love life." I think the future looks good, but we must remember that the fruit only comes when we have had time to sow the seeds and bring in the harvest. It may be some time before many of us see how the world reacts. Maybe a lot of what is being done now is simply reclaiming the living seeds. It is these living seeds that will germinate and flower again.

PART THREE

STRATEGIES OF
RESISTANCE

12

A SMALL PLACE

− Jamaica Kincaid −

IF YOU GO TO Antigua as a tourist, this is what you will see. If you come by aeroplane, you will land at the V. C. Bird International Airport. Vere Cornwall (V. C.) Bird is the Prime Minister of Antigua. You may be the sort of tourist who would wonder why a Prime Minister would want an airport named after him—why not a school, why not a hospital, why not some great public monument? You are a tourist and you have not yet seen a school in Antigua, you have not yet seen the hospital in Antigua, you have not yet seen a public monument in Antigua. As your plane descends to land, you might say, What a beautiful island Antigua is—more beautiful than any of the other islands you have seen, and they were very beautiful, in their way, but they were much too green, much too lush with vegetation, which indicated to you, the tourist, that they got quite a bit of rainfall, and rain is the very thing that you, just now, do not want, for you are thinking of the hard and cold and dark and long days you spent working in North America (or, worse, Europe), earning some money so that you could stay in this place (Antigua) where the sun always shines and where the climate is deliciously hot and dry for the four to ten days you are going to be staying there; and since you are on your holiday, since you are a tourist, the thought of what it might be like for someone who had to live day in, day out in a place that suffers constantly from drought, and so has to watch carefully every drop of fresh water used (while at the same time surrounded by a sea and an ocean—the Caribbean Sea on one side, the Atlantic Ocean on the other), must never cross your mind.

You disembark your plane. You go through customs. Since you are a tourist, a North American or European—to be frank, white— and not an Antiguan black returning to Antigua from Europe or North America with cardboard boxes of much needed cheap clothes and food for relatives, you move through customs swiftly, you move through customs with ease. Your bags are not searched. You emerge from customs into the hot, clean air: immediately you feel cleansed, immediately you feel blessed (which is to say special); you feel free. You see a man, a taxi driver; you ask him to take you to your destination; he quotes you a price. You immediately think that the price is in the local currency, for you are a tourist and you are familiar with these things (rates of exchange) and you feel even more free, for things seem so cheap, but then your driver ends by saying, "In US currency." You may say, "Hmmmm, do you have a formal sheet that lists official prices and destinations?" Your driver obeys the law and shows you the sheet, and he apologizes for the incredible mistake he has made in quoting you a price off the top of his head which is so vastly different (favoring him) from the one listed. You are driven to your hotel by this taxi driver in his taxi, a brand-new Japanese-made vehicle. The road on which you are travelling is a very bad road, very much in need of repair. You are feeling wonderful, so you say, "Oh, what a marvellous change these bad roads are from the splendid highways I am used to in North America." (Or, worse, Europe.) Your driver is reckless; he is a dangerous man who drives in the middle of the road when he thinks no other cars are coming in the opposite direction, passes other cars on blind curves that run uphill, drives at sixty miles an hour on narrow, curving roads when the road sign, a rusting, beat-up thing left over from colonial days, says 40 MPH. This might frighten you (you are on your holiday; you are a tourist); this might excite you (you are on your holiday; you are a tourist), though if you are from New York and take taxis you are used to this style of driving: most of the taxi drivers in New York are from places in the world like this. You are looking out the window (because you want to get your money's worth); you notice that all the cars you see are brand-new, or almost brand-new, and that they are all Japanese-made. There are no American cars in Antigua—no new ones, at any rate; none that were manufactured in the last ten years. You continue to look at the cars and you say to yourself, Why, they look brand-new, but they have an awful sound, like an old car—a very old, dilapidated car. How to account for that? Well, possibly it's because they use leaded gasoline in these brand-new cars whose engines were built to use non-leaded gasoline, but you musn't ask the person driving the car if this is so, because he or she has never heard of unleaded gasoline. You look closely at the car; you see that it's a model of a Japanese car that you might hesitate to buy; it's a model that's very expensive; it's a model that's quite impractical for a person who has to work as hard as you do and who watches every penny you earn so that you can afford this holiday you are on. How do they afford such a car? And do they live in a luxurious house to match such a car? Well, no. You will be surprised, then, to see that most likely the person driving this brand-new car filled with the wrong gas lives in a house that, in comparison, is far beneath the status of the car; and if you were to ask why you would be told that the banks are encouraged by the government to make loans available for cars, but loans for houses not so easily available; and if you ask again why, you will be told that the two main car dealerships in Antigua are owned in part or outright by ministers in government. Oh, but you are on holiday and the sight of these brand-new cars driven by people who may or may not have really passed their driving test (there was once a scandal about driving licenses for sale) would not really stir up these thoughts in you. You pass a building sitting in a sea of dust and you think, It's some latrines for people just passing by, but when you look again you see the building has written on it PIGOTT'S SCHOOL. You pass the hospital, the Holberton Hospital, and how wrong you are not to think about this, for though you are a tourist on your holiday, what if your heart should miss a few beats? What if a blood vessel in your neck should break? What if one of those people driving those brand-new cars filled with the wrong gas fails to pass safely while going uphill on a curve and you are in the car going in the opposite direction? Will you be comforted to know that the hospital is staffed with doctors that no actual Antiguan trusts; that Antiguans always say about the doctors, "I don't want them near me"; that Antiguans refer to them not as doctors but as "the three men" (there are three of them); that when the Minister of Health himself doesn't feel well he takes the first plane to New York to see a real doctor; that if any one of the ministers in government needs medical care he flies to New York to get it?

It's a good thing that you brought your own books with you, for you couldn't just go to the library and borrow some. Antigua used to have a splendid library, but in The Earthquake (everyone talks about it that way—The Earthquake; we Antiguans, for I am one, have a great sense of things, and the more meaningful the thing, the more meaningless we make it) the library building was damaged. This was in 1974, and soon after that a sign was placed on the front of the building saying, THIS BUILDING WAS DAMAGED IN THE EARTHQUAKE OF 1974. REPAIRS ARE PENDING. The sign hangs there, and hangs there more than a decade later, with its unfulfilled promise of repair, and you might see this as a sort of quaintness on the part of these islanders, these people descended from slaves—what a strange, unusual perception of time they have. REPAIRS ARE PENDING, and here it is many years later, but perhaps in a world that is twelve miles long and nine miles wide (the size of Antigua) twelve years and twelve minutes and twelve days are all the same. The library is one of those splendid old buildings from colonial times, and the sign telling of the repairs is a splendid old sign from colonial times. Not very long after The Earthquake Antigua got its independence from Britain, making Antigua a state in its own right, and Antiguans are so proud of this that each year, to mark the day, they go to church and thank God, a British God, for this. But you should not think of the confusion that must lie in all that and you must not think of the damaged library. You have brought your own books with you, and among them is one of those new books about economic history, one of those books explaining how the West (meaning Europe and North America after its conquest and settlement by Europeans) got rich: the West got rich not from the free (free—in this case meaning got-for-nothing) and then undervalued labour, for generations, of the people like me you see walking around you in Antigua but from the ingenuity of small shopkeepers in Sheffield and Yorkshire and Lancashire, or wherever; and what a great part the invention of the wristwatch played in it, for there was nothing noble-minded men could not do when they discovered they could slap time on their wrists just like that (isn't that the last straw; for not only did we have to suffer the unspeakableness of slavery, but the satisfaction to be had from "We made you bastards rich" is taken away, too), and so you needn't let that slightly funny feeling you have from time to time about exploitation, oppression, domination develop into full-fledged unease, discomfort; you could ruin your holiday. They are not responsible for what you have; you owe them nothing; in fact, you did them a big favour, and you can provide one hundred examples.

For here you are now, passing by Government House. And here you are now, passing by the Prime Minister's Office and the Parliament Building, and overlooking these, with a splendid view of St. John's Harbour, the American Embassy. If it were not for you, they would not have Government House, and Prime Minister's Office, and Parliament Building and embassy of powerful country. Now you are passing a mansion, an extraordinary house painted the colour of old cow dung, with more aerials and antennas attached to it than you will see even at the American Embassy. The people who live in this house are a merchant family who came to Antigua from the Middle East less than twenty years ago. When this family first came to Antigua, they sold dry goods door to door from suitcases they carried on their backs. Now they own a lot of Antigua; they regularly lend money to the government, they build enormous (for Antigua), ugly (for Antigua), concrete buildings in Antigua's capital, St. John's, which the government then rents for huge sums of money; a member of their family is the Antiguan Ambassador to Syria; Antiguans hate them. Not far from this mansion is another mansion, the home of a drug smuggler. Everybody knows he's a drug smuggler, and if just as you were driving by he stepped out of his door your driver might point him out to you as the notorious person that he is, for this drug smuggler is so rich people say he buys cars in tens—ten of this one, ten of that one—and that he bought a house (another mansion) near Five Islands, contents included, with cash he carried in a suitcase: three hundred and fifty thousand American dollars, and, to the surprise of the seller of the house, lots of American dollars were left over. Overlooking the drug smuggler's mansion is yet another mansion, and leading up to it is the best paved road in all of Antigua—even better than the road that was paved for the Queen's visit in 1985 (when the Queen came, all the roads that she would travel on were paved anew, so that the Queen might have been left with the impression that riding in a car in Antigua was a pleasant experience). In this mansion lives a woman sophisticated people in Antigua call Evita. She is a notorious woman. She's young and beautiful and the girlfriend of somebody very high up in the government. Evita is notorious because her relationship with this high government official has made her the owner of boutiques and property and given her a say in cabinet meetings, and all sorts of other privileges such a relationship would bring a beautiful young woman.

Oh, but by now you are tired of all this looking, and you want to reach your destination—your hotel, your room. You long to refresh yourself; you long to eat some nice lobster, some nice local food. You take a bath, you brush your teeth. You get dressed again; as you get dressed, you look out the window. That water—have you ever seen anything like it? Far out, to the horizon, the colour of the water is navy-blue; nearer, the water is the colour of the North American sky. From there to the shore, the water is pale, silvery, clear, so clear that you can see its pinkish-white sand bottom. Oh, what beauty! Oh, what beauty! You have never seen anything like this. You are so excited. You breathe shallow. You breathe deep. You see a beautiful boy skimming the water, godlike, on a Windsurfer. You see an incredibly unattractive, fat, pastrylike-fleshed woman enjoying a walk on the beautiful sand with a man, an incredibly unattractive, fat, pastrylike-fleshed man; you see the pleasure they're taking in their surroundings. Still standing, looking out the window, you see yourself lying on the beach, enjoying the amazing sun (a sun so powerful and yet so beautiful, the way it is always overhead as if on permanent guard, ready to stamp out any cloud that dares to darken and so empty rain on you and ruin your holiday; a sun that is your personal friend). You see yourself taking a walk on that beach, you see yourself meeting new people (only they are new in a very limited way, for they are people just like you). You see yourself eating some delicious, locally grown food. You see yourself, you see yourself . . . You must not wonder what exactly happened to the contents of your lavatory when you flushed it. You must not wonder where your bathwater went when you pulled out the stopper. You must not wonder what happened when you brushed your teeth. Oh, it might all end up in the water you are thinking of taking a swim in; the contents of your lavatory might, just might, graze gently against your ankle as you wade carefree in the water, for you see, in Antigua, there is no proper sewage-disposal system. But the Caribbean Sea is very big and the Atlantic Ocean is even bigger; it would amaze even you to know the number of black slaves this ocean has swallowed up. When you sit down to eat your delicious meal, it's better that you don't know that most of what you are eating came off a plane from Miami. And before it got on a plane in Miami, who knows where it came from? A good guess is that it came from a place like Antigua first, where it was grown dirt-cheap, went to Miami, and came back. There is a world of something in this, but I can't go into it right now.

The thing you have always suspected about yourself the minute you become a tourist is true: A tourist is an ugly human being. You are not an ugly person all the time; you are not an ugly person ordinarily; you are not an ugly person day to day. From day to day, you are a nice person. From day to day, all the people who are supposed to love you on the whole do. From day to day, as you walk down a busy street in the large and modern and prosperous city in which you work and live, dismayed, puzzled (a cliché, but only a cliché can explain you) at how alone you feel in this crowd, how awful it is to go unnoticed, how awful it is to go unloved, even as you are surrounded by more people than you could possibly get to know in a lifetime that lasted for millennia, and then out of the corner of your eye you see someone looking at you and absolute pleasure is written all over that person's face, and then you realize that you are not as revolting a presence as you think you are (for that look just told you so). And so, ordinarily, you are a nice person, an attractive person, a person capable of drawing to yourself the affection of other people (people just like you), a person at home in your own skin (sort of; I mean, in a way; I mean, your dismay and puzzlement are natural to you, because people like you just seem to be like that, and so many of the things people like you find admirable about yourselves—the things you think about, the things you think really define you—seem rooted in these feelings): a person at home in your own house (and all its nice house things), with its nice back yard (and its nice back-yard things), at home on your street, your church, in community activities, your job, at home with your family, your relatives, your friends—you are a whole person. But one day, when you are sitting somewhere, alone in that crowd, and that awful feeling of displacedness comes over you, and really, as an ordinary person you are not well equipped to look too far inward and set yourself aright, because being ordinary is already so taxing, and being ordinary takes all you have out of you, and though the words "I must get away" do not actually pass across your lips, you make a leap from being that nice blob just sitting like a boob in your amniotic sac of the modern experience to being a person visiting heaps of death and ruin and feeling alive and inspired at the sight of it; to being a person lying on some far-away beach, your stilled body stinking and glistening in the sand, looking like something first forgotten, then remembered, then not important enough to go back for; to being a person marvelling at the harmony (ordinarily, what you would say is the backwardness) and the union these other people (and they are other people) have with nature. And you look at the things they can do with a piece of ordinary cloth, the things they fashion out of cheap, vulgarly colored (to you) twine, the way they squat down over a hole they have made in the ground, the hole itself is something to marvel at, and since you are being an ugly person this ugly but joyful thought will swell inside you: their ancestors were not clever in the way yours were and not ruthless in the way yours were, for then would it not be you who would be in harmony with nature and backwards in that charming way? An ugly thing, that is what you are when you become a tourist, an ugly, empty thing, a stupid thing, a piece of rubbish pausing here and there to gaze at this and taste that, and it will never occur to you that the people who inhabit the place in which you have just paused cannot stand you, that behind their closed doors they laugh at your strangeness (you do not look the way they look); the physical sight of you does not please them; you have bad manners (it is their custom to eat their food with their hands; you try eating their way, you look silly; you try eating the way you always eat, you look silly); they do not like the way you speak (you have an accent); they collapse helpless from laughter, mimicking the way they imagine you must look as you carry out some everyday bodily function. They do not like you. They do not like me! That thought never actually occurs to you. Still, you feel a little uneasy. Still, you feel a little foolish. Still, you feel a little out of place. But the banality of your own life is very real to you; it drove you to this extreme, spending your days and your nights in the company of people who despise you, people you do not like really, people you would not want to have as your actual neighbour. And so you must devote yourself to puzzling out how much of what you are told is really, really true (Is ground-up bottle glass in peanut sauce really a delicacy around here, or will it do just what you think ground-up bottle glass will do? Is this rare, multicoloured, snout-mouthed fish really an aphrodisiac, or will it cause you to fall asleep permanently?). Oh, the hard work all of this is, and is it any wonder, then, that on your return home you feel the need of a long rest, so that you can recover from your life as a tourist?

That the native does not like the tourist is not hard to explain. For every native of every place is a potential tourist, and every tourist is a native of somewhere. Every native everywhere lives a life of overwhelming and crushing banality and boredom and desperation and depression, and every deed, good and bad, is an attempt to forget this. Every native would like to find a way out, every native would like a rest, every native would like a tour. But some natives—most natives in the world—cannot go anywhere. They are too poor. They are too poor to go anywhere. They are too poor to escape the reality of their lives; and they are too poor to live properly in the place where they live, which is the very place you, the tourist, want to go—so when the natives see you, the tourist, they envy you, they envy your ability to leave your own banality and boredom, they envy your ability to turn their own banality and boredom into a source of pleasure for yourself.

13

ONE PRECIOUS MOMENT

– Margaret Randall –

1.

Could we have imagined a world more rife with horror, more submerged in chaos, more blighted by injustice of all types, than the one we inhabit at this beginning of the twenty-first century? Could we have predicted a world in which those who rule are so utterly consumed by greed, so power hungry yet so protected, so careless and seemingly oblivious to the ways in which what they perpetrate today will affect all future life?

The arrogance and isolationism with which the George W. Bush administration has decided to formally renounce any involvement in an international criminal court, has declared it will no longer be bound by the 1969 Vienna Convention on the Law of Treaties, and has continued to ignore the Kyoto accords on the reduction of greenhouse gases, shouts a single message: We don't care!

Who, even a few years back, could have imagined a government openly making vicious war against an already devastated land, while at the same time dropping food packages that look like land mines and asking school children to send dollar bills to their counterparts in that far-off country? The United States has a long history of such assaults, but until fairly recently the US people still had the capacity to be shocked—so the operations were carried out covertly. Until fairly recently, today's images would have been discarded as absurd, even by those Madison Avenue experts whose job it is to convince us of all manner of absurdity; even now when information and disinformation are played as entertainment rather than news.

Those brave men and women who struggle against the perpetrators—demonstrating in the streets of Seattle and Genoa, showing up by the tens of thousands in Porto Alegre, or working for peace and an equitable distribution of goods and services in their own communities—wage the good fight. In terms of power, they are horribly disadvantaged. Most target a piece of the whole, and don't stand much of a chance when confronted with today's hegemony.

So I know that I leave myself open to every sort of critique when I say that I dream a simple solution. Terrifyingly, beautifully simple. I suggest that if each of us were committed to a full measure of justice for every other being, and did our part as well to care for our earth, air, water, and other resources, the problems that confront us would fade. That simple. But that terrifying.

I dream, sometimes, of a modern day Lysistrata, but much more complete. Not a withholding of sex alone, but of any sort of cooperation with those who are doing such a thorough job of destroying our nest and all who inhabit it.

I say the simple solution terrifies, because it is clear to me that what I perceive as obvious will not, cannot, come about. It would require a childlike recognition, a turn of heart and mind impossible for those who hold the reins, impossible even for those who truly *want* such a change but can only think in terms of globalization, the liberalization of markets, what must be on the next agenda for this or that summit, how to lobby or promote, coerce or convince.

In Cuba billboards often bore the admonition: "If you know, teach. If you don't know, learn." Simple as that. Each of us doing our part on the world stage or in the relationship, family, community, workplace, or school. This is the sort of simplicity I am thinking of: individually and collectively learning to see the other, reject concepts and ideologies that minimize the other's rights, and assume responsible stewardship wherever we may be.

I didn't always feel this way. Not that many years back, in fact, I would have scoffed at such a seemingly simplistic suggestion. But now I say that the simple solution is beautiful because of its simplicity, like a mathematical model in which every question has been elegantly addressed. What is simple is too often overlooked. This, then, is the story of how my vision of the world has simultaneously become simpler and more complex, more complete. I want to explore how my sojourn in Mexico, Cuba, and Nicaragua has affected my North American social conditioning, my understanding of disenfranchisement and human rights.

2.

I was born in 1936. From an early age, something—I still don't know exactly what—made justice important to me. My parents preached honesty and fairness, though as our family life unfolded I, like those in every generation, came to understand that their ideas of honesty and fairness were limited by their own needs, prejudices, and fears. I am a product of the North American middle class, privileged by race, disadvantaged by gender—and, much later, also by sexual identity.

My own early ideas of justice were limited too. I thought African Americans were treated poorly, but I was almost completely alienated from the Mexican Americans who lived downtown in my own southwestern city. My friends and I referred to them as *pachucos*. I imagined their greased pompadours held hidden knives.

My mother and father seemed fascinated by Native Americans, and we periodically took old clothing out to the pueblos to trade for silver and turquoise jewelry. I was only vaguely uncomfortable with this practice; I certainly didn't grasp the ugliness of bartering throwaway clothes for family heirlooms.

I had other confusing exposures. My father taught music in the public schools and had the summers off, so we took freighters to South America and listened to him read us *The Father Brown Stories* while picnicking in English poppy fields. Those journeys expanded my sense of the world, but in retrospect, I've wished our parents had been politically astute enough to be able to transmit a more complex sense of what life was like for the people we met.

In the fifties, no one I knew spoke openly about homosexuality, so despite the fact that my aunt and her partner lived in Santa Fe and we visited them often, I was unable to think of lesbians and gay men as real. Homophobic and racist allusions and jokes were part of my parents' discourse, mild when compared to some, but homophobic and racist, nevertheless. When confronted, they denied the implications. They didn't think of themselves as racist, classist, or prejudiced in any sense. Yet my mother's response whenever I made a grammatical error—or fell into the New York accent that was my birthright—was always, "You speak like a Brooklyn shop girl."

It took me many years to understand that this response was not only classist, but also anti-Semitic. Just after I was born, my parents changed our surname from Reinthal to Randall. My repeated questions as to why, invariably brought answers like "Oh, it's easier to spell" or "We just didn't care for your grandparents' values." It wasn't until after my father's death in 1994 that my mother admitted she had suffered anti-Semitic jibes as a young girl. "I never wanted my children to suffer that," she said. I knew that major US universities still had quotas for Jews at the time my father got his degree. If our parents had been able to share their pain and fear instead of lying to us, my early years at least would have felt a lot less confusing.

Although I certainly couldn't have articulated it then, I have come to understand that the justice I hoped for and sought as a child was reserved for white Anglo-Saxon men. As a young woman, I too easily accepted the expectations and morality that placed me and other females in positions subservient to the men in our lives. Although intellectually I believed that non-white men and women deserved fair treatment, I had not yet examined my own racism. Practically speaking, as a young person I knew few people unlike myself.

Still, I saw myself as someone concerned with fairness and, within my limitations of class and color and culture, I was. As a young person, I knew I would be a writer. Making the creative journey undoubtedly provided me with a context in which justice seemed a laudable thing. Would I have developed in the same way had I sought a career in business or politics? I don't know.

3.

In my early twenties I spent several intense years in New York City among the abstract expressionist artists who were seeking to invent an American school of painting and among poets seeking authentic patterns of American speech. Some of these people were what our culture likes to call apolitical; process was more important to them than content, social or any other. But some—among them mentors like Elaine de Kooning, Jerome Rothenberg, Joel Oppenheimer, Walter Lowenfels, Nancy Macdonald, Allen Ginsberg, Ammon Hennacy, Milton Resnick, and Pat Passlof—were always engaged with the important issues of their times. Those who didn't explicitly paint or write about those issues, organized, demonstrated, signed petitions, stood at the barricades.

I thought of myself as independent, because I lived alone, supported myself, made my own decisions, but it was a mediated independence. Many, although certainly not all, of the young women in the New York art world of those years were "group-ies," following and catering to the men rather than prioritizing our own creative visions.

In those late fifties, McCarthyism still chilled our nation's creativity. Artists and writers I knew had been persecuted by the witch hunts, their lives broken. Others, whom I knew only through their work, lost jobs, were imprisoned, gave or refused to give names. Fear stalked us all. Creative people were particularly vulnerable.

Career jobs—in the academy, on the important journals, in museums and galleries—went to those artists who were politically safe. What saved us in the subsequent generations was our rebellion and our talent.

I left New York City in the fall of 1960. My painter and poet colleagues and I moved off in different directions. They remained in a world defined by art. I entered one defined by art and politics. The lines were more fluid than this, of course, but the emphasis was important. Years later, an old New York City friend told me: "You coped by leaving, I coped by staying." She was talking about our lives as women and also as political and artistic beings.

I went to Mexico, and quickly fell in with other expatriates from the United States and from several Latin American countries. In New York I had become a single mother. With my young son, I reinvented myself in a country it would take me years to know and whose language I was only beginning to learn. Never one to move away from a challenge, I threw myself into the fray: late-night poetry salons in two languages, a politics of anti-imperialism, a man I would soon marry, and the dream of a bilingual literary journal that would become a culturally rich and influential institution.

The decade of the sixties in Mexico put me in contact with writers and artists throughout the world, all working through their own personal or collective rejections of establishment conditioning. I learned that one could write or paint or sculpt or dance or sing or make theater about anything that touched one's spirit, desire, rage. Not only that one could, but that one *had* to write about what was vital, what was integral to one's holistic sense of self. Form and content had begun to merge.

Those were years of an extraordinary creative renaissance, one in which art and progressive ideas—political, economic, psychological, sociological—came together in new directions and forms. The man I married seemed the opposite of those free spirits I'd left behind in New York. But then, those men had only really felt free to fulfill their own aspirations, not mine. And neither they nor I knew how to talk about the problem. I mistook Sergio's possessive jealousy for love, at least for a while. It wasn't until he joined a cult that proclaimed quite unequivocally that women could not attain nirvana that I began to understand how deep the woman-hate ran.

Our arrival in Mexico at the end of 1960, and the repression of the 1968 uprising that changed that country and me, became parenthetical bookends to a particularly intense period of my life. Sergio Mondragón and I married and had two daughters, Sarah and Ximena. We divorced in 1968, and the following year—with US poet Robert Cohen—I had another daughter, Ana. *El Corno Emplumado/The Plumed Horn*, the literary journal I founded with Sergio, ran for thirty-one issues and was one of the defining forums for the work of many up-and-coming writers and artists in North and Latin America—as well as to a lesser extent throughout the rest of the world.

I had also grown in my ability to incorporate new human groups into my personal "family of man"—and I use the word *man* intentionally. Long gone were the days when Albuquerque's downtown Mexican Americans frightened me; my own family was now thoroughly Latin Americanized and I myself had become a "hybrid"—reading and speaking Spanish as easily as English.

During this time, the Cuban Revolution also became part of my life. I traveled to Cuba first in January of 1967, again at the beginning of 1968, and—when political repression finally made it necessary for me to flee Mexico—my family and I moved there in the fall of 1969. The revolution's first two decades were magical, transforming. Now I was able to stretch my concepts of justice further, and also take note of the challenges inherent in exchanging the old, stratified social patterns for new, more egalitarian ones.

4.

Cuba initiated a new chapter in my creative life. By this time I had discovered feminism, and as with all intellectual or spiritual discoveries, I began looking at my own life in the context of feminist ideas. My poetry—my writing in general—became more consciously female, more proud of my condition as a woman with a gender-specific take on life. Now I wrote not only as a socialist, and as a hybrid North and Latin American, but also as a woman—of a particular culture, class, and experience.

My children reaped the wonders (and sometimes also the rigors) of a Cuban education. I was supported in my desire to write about Cuban women: to learn the skills of an oral historian and to listen to women who had become the protagonists of their own lives tell their stories of that experience. Most important, for eleven years and as one more worker-mother-poet, I participated in all aspects of one of the great social experiments of our time, one that despite its problems and setbacks continues to be an example.

I met other poets—from Cuba and many countries of the world. I read Angolan and Palestinian poetry for the first time, and memorized some of Nazim Hikmet and Bertolt Brecht's poems, all in Spanish translation. I learned to read César Vallejo in his original, language-changing tongue. I learned about how creative people organize in a socialist society, joined discussions about what rights and obligations artists have, reveled in a culture that loves and respects creative endeavor and supports its creative spirits.

I value my participation in many of the official Cuban artistic programs of those years. But one experience that stands out is an unofficial effort. During my last few years on the island, a dozen or so other poets and I met each Saturday morning at a spot on the campus of the University of Havana known as El Rincón de los Cabezones—Big Head Corner. Beneath the grotesque busts of great (male) intellects, we read and critiqued one another's work. We called our workshop El taller Roque Dalton, after the great Salvadoran poet who had also been a friend.

Although I was prone to incorporate into my living the lessons of whatever idea sparked my interest, there was often some distance between idea and assimilation. I still hung out mostly with male poets and writers. Male voices and visions had been overwhelming in the sections of *El Corno Emplumado* dedicated to Cuban work, as in the journal overall. Once in Cuba, my 1978 anthology of young Cuban poets included a couple of women in a mostly male selection. By 1982 I understood the ways in which I had been shaped by my own prejudices and made up for this with the first bilingual anthology of twentieth-century Cuban women poets.

I was also taking a closer look at my home life. When Robert and I met and fell in love in Mexico, he seemed very different from Sergio: a man who had been consumed by an anguish he too often took out on me. By comparison, Robert seemed transparent: honest, capable, strong. Younger than I, he was more a product of the hippie generation than the beats, a smart New Yorker who read Wittgenstein, wanted an open relationship, and scorned those who were not like him. I left Sergio, grateful to be free of that intense self-hate, and initiated the relationship with Robert, eager for what

I thought would be a more egalitarian, more intellectually and politically stimulating arrangement.

The problem was, I didn't yet know how to love myself. I didn't yet know who this woman I needed to love was. And I was more and more deeply involved with revolutionary movements and organizations that shunned personal reflection. Self-examination was perceived of as "bourgeois deviancy." For a middle-class white woman like myself, it was only too easy to push the personal questions down. But Robert and I, like Sergio and I, were linked by poetry, by our creative spirits and passion to change the world. We loved our children. And we engaged in the battles around household division of labor, monogamy vs. nonmonogamy, and the basic issues of trust that characterized our generation.

Like many in my children's generation, two of my daughters feel my struggle to make the world better for all children prevented me from spending time with them. They berate me for this much more than they do their fathers. Only my son speaks of a fully satisfying childhood. My youngest daughter feels she lacked a real childhood, knew what we, her parents, "liked her to do—and they were all grown up things." How women of my generation who were involved in revolutionary struggle mothered, is clearly a sore point for our offspring—and for us. Although I am close to all my children, regret and pain often accompany my own memories of mothering.

By the end of the seventies, my life in Cuba had begun to unravel. I had learned a great deal about how a small nation can try to change its political, economic, and social reality. And I had learned, firsthand, about the obstacles. Some of the lessons, and many of the people, will be with me forever. I will always be grateful for the ways in which Cuba embraced my children and me, what it gave us, the audacity, dignity, courage, and creativity I witnessed.

At the same time, my rebellious nature had entered into conflict with certain aspects of an authoritarian and essentially male-dominated state. I had left Robert a couple of years before, and was now living with a poet, musician, and ex-guerrilla from Venezuela, Antonio Castro. Antonio was a kind and gentle man: devoted, loyal. From an impoverished background and after five years in prison, his values were solid. But now this relationship too had played itself out. I accepted an invitation to visit Nicaragua during the last three months of 1979—to research and write a book about that country's women—and I eventually moved there at the end of 1980.

5.

I went to Nicaragua with my youngest daughter, Ana, who was 10 at the time. My son and two older daughters elected to remain in Cuba, although Ximena joined us in Managua when she graduated from high school the following year. Some of the young Sandinistas, then making a revolution unnoticed by most outside of Central America, had spent periods of time in Cuba throughout the seventies and several had become close friends. So when we arrived in Nicaragua we had privileged contacts, and I found myself in on the ground floor of an experiment in social change that was vibrant and in many ways more open-ended than what I had experienced in Cuba.

In 1969, when I'd gone to live in Cuba, that country's revolution was already ten years old. It was set in many of its ways. Its socialism, although uniquely Cuban, was also inevitably influenced by the more classically Marxist views of the international Communist movement, especially the privileging of class over any of society's other contradictions. This relegated women to a place where equality in education and work were believed sufficient to effect lasting change.

When I went to Nicaragua in 1979 to work on the book, and again at the end of 1980 to live, everything was new. Anything seemed possible. Nicaragua also bore the distinction of being a nation of poets. Artistic creativity is deeply respected there. Many of the poets and artists, as well as those men—and the occasional woman—in charge of the new government, were my friends. Many of the new government officials were also serious writers.

During my four years in Nicaragua, I worked at the new Ministry of Culture, with the women's organization, with the Union of Artists and Writers, and for the ideological department of the FSLN (Frente Sandinista de Liberación Nacional). I witnessed and was part of a multifaceted artistic outreach. Women continued to be in the forefront of my concern, and I wrote several books about the ongoing struggles of Nicaraguan women to gain true equality in the revolutionary, and postrevolutionary, society. I also wrote about Nicaraguan writers, and about the unique relationship between religious faith and revolution, something I had not seen in Cuba.

My experience with Liberation Theology changed me in important ways. I never became a believer, but the progressive Catholic communities taught me that compassion and a deeper introspection about self were not contradictions in the struggle to remake society. In fact, both are necessary to that struggle, if it is to address the needs of the whole community.

Two decades separated the Cuban and Nicaraguan victories, two decades that were particularly important in twentieth century history. The 1959 victory of the Cuban revolution predated the revival of feminist thought and practice internationally (what some have called the second wave of feminism); it was also pre-Vatican II, the powerful movement for change within the Catholic Church. Both these events would exert important influences upon the FSLN during its ten years in power.

They were important, as well, in shaping women's experience. It is unnecessary to explain why this was true of feminism. Vatican II made a difference in women's lives because Christian culture and morality had conditioned and thwarted those lives throughout the Christian world, and a more liberal reading of the relationship between the Church and its people opened previously unheard of opportunities for women. A number of women achieved important positions while the Sandinistas were in power; many more, while not center stage, made the revolution possible. Their stories amazed me. Their strength and refusal to retreat into traditional women's roles had me—and many others—believing that life was changing for women in dramatic and irreversible ways.

Eventually, in Sandinista Nicaragua as in Fidel's Cuba, the men in power balked at women's attempts to have meaningful input into any decision making that challenged the power equilibrium. I believe that the inability to look honestly at the issue of gender equality was at least partially responsible for the 1990 Sandinista electoral defeat, just as it prevents the Cuban government from making structural changes that would grant more power to women.

This issue is not central to the story I'm telling here, though it's been examined in other essays. Suffice it to say that a number of Nicaraguan women became important mentors to me: Doris Tijerino, Dora María Téllez, Sofía Montenegro, María López Vigíl, and others. Although they have lost much of what they fought so hard to build, their stories continue to inspire me.

6.

In 1984 I returned to the United States. I had lived in Latin America for close to a quarter century. I was exhausted, in need of reconnecting to my roots, and eager to understand how the various strands of my experience combined in the woman I had become.

Over the next years I would focus on the desert landscape of my youth, my newfound woman-loving self, psychotherapy that helped uncover an experience of incest in my early childhood, life without my children, and an almost five-year deportation battle with the US Immigration and Naturalization Service because of opinions expressed in some of my books.

This is when my world split open. Male-dominated organizations and institutions no longer limited my vision or sense of self. The US women's movement, and within it a confident lesbian community, welcomed me home—to my country and my individuality. The deep understanding of international political and economic domination, shaped and sharpened during my years in Latin America, remained indelible. To that I now added a merging of mind and body, a new openness to humans in all our magnificent difference, and an awareness of the importance of protecting resources I had long taken for granted. I touched a cultural taproot, long ignored, of language and image, sound and feeling. And there was the desert, the New Mexican desert, where as a teenager I had followed the wavy lines of Geological Survey maps as I explored earth, space, light, time.

I hadn't understood how much I needed this, my original landscape. Or how much reconnecting with it would lead me back to myself. My body was there, waiting to be used. I had never used it, not really: moving from shy and awkward teenager to sedentary writer. My lasting partner—a woman—slowly coaxed me into walking, hiking, biking. She never derided, always encouraged. And it was on the desert and in the mountains of New Mexico that I discovered not only my own muscle and reach but the diamondback basking in the sun, the deer standing silent on the trail, the gift of a coyote bounding across the road, birds and bears and bobcats.

Had I been born into a family that sought its sustenance from the land, that looked of necessity to rain and rock and soil and the animals that call these home, I might have learned earlier that I am part of nature, and to care about the lives of all creatures and natural elements rather than prioritizing one species over others. Since I was not, I needed the luxury of time and age to learn to appreciate these other inhabitants. I remember a good friend, in the seventies, who was almost embarrassed to tell me she was going out on a ship to save the whales. Correctly, she assumed I would belittle her concern for whales when so many humans were besieged by hunger, violence, war. My friend died more than a decade ago. I wish I could tell her I finally understand.

7.

During my first years back in the US, my immigration case highlighted issues of artistic expression vis-à-vis love of country, an artist's rights and obligations, and how the US power structure perceives women, punishing without apology those who challenge government policy. I learned how one manages prolonged political struggle while maintaining one's integrity. With the help of good lawyers, supportive family, and many, many friends—artists, writers, performers, political activists, unionists, religious people, women and men, lesbian, gay, and straight, academics, and others—I won my immigration case in August 1989.

Now I was free to remain in the country of my birth, specifically among the red rock mountains, canyons, and desert of my adolescence. I began to notice and enjoy nature, explore my relationship to it. Seasons of chamisa. Desert flowers. These images found their way into my poetry, along with the human stories, and the newer, more complex emotions. I found the love of a woman who has been my partner for the past eighteen years, a love relationship posited on each encouraging the growth of the other, a relationship that will endure. I began to deal with the scars of childhood sexual abuse. I began to grow old—if not gracefully, at least with a welcome sense of wholeness.

This sense of wholeness, however, seemed to develop in opposition to a rapidly deteriorating national and global political situation. Forced to wage my immigration battle under the Reagan and elder Bush presidencies, I remember wishing I had been able to do so under Carter. Now I understand that under the George W. Bush/Cheney/Ashcroft administration, I would almost certainly have been deported. Government policies that remained covert twenty years ago are now carried out overtly. The wanton invasion of other countries and reversal of civil liberties here at home—both under the rubric of "fighting terrorism"—have become ordinary and acceptable to most Americans.

I used to believe that poetry could save the world. By save the world, I didn't mean in the Christian definition of salvation. I meant that poetry—the power of words, their energy and ability to ignite our clarity and tenderness, our deepest feelings and most elevated intelligence—is capable of freeing us from complacency and turning us toward an understanding of what is necessary for our survival and healthy growth.

Today I don't know if I believe that poetry can save the world. I am appalled as each new day brings another example of arrogance, abuse of power, deceit, greed run wild, and gross distortion of this system we continue to call a democracy. The disintegration of so many dreams and the failures within our own movements for social change have left me unsteady on my previously sure feet.

What I do know, what I know more completely than I ever have, is that one precious moment is capable of effecting a change of heart or will, of opening eyes or taking the wanderer by the hand. The writer Barbara Kingsolver, wandering with her husband in the Costa Rican countryside, has attempted to describe this moment of truth, which occurs most often when we take time out from our rage or terror to notice the way creatures in nature go about their elegant business of life. In her encounter with a flock of scarlet macaws, Kingsolver finds hope for the future:

> All afternoon we walked crook-necked and openmouthed with awe. If these creatures are doomed, they don't act that way: *El que quiera azul celesle, que le cueste,* but who could buy or possess such avian magnificence against the blue sky? We stopped counting at 50. We'd have settled for just one—that was what we thought we had come for—but we stayed through the change of tide and nearly till sunset because of the way they perched and foraged and spoke among themselves, without a care for a human's expectations. What held us there was the show of pure, defiant survival: this audacious thing with feathers, this hope.[1]

Maybe this is the cornerstone with which we must continually create a knowledge that will compel us to face our alternatives: Embrace all creatures and elements or hasten annihilation. The terrifyingly, beautifully simple answer. Poetry must become the word that saves—not for some mythical invention of afterlife or glory, but for the here and now of who we are and can be.

NOTES

1. Barbara Kingsolver, *Small Wonder: Essays* (New York: HarperCollins, 2002), 59.

14

ON BEING SHORTER

How Our Testimonial Texts Defy the Academy

– Alicia Partnoy –

No one can live
with a death inside: you have to choose between
tossing it far away
like a rotten fruit
or keeping it
and dying from contamination.

—Alaíde Foppa

I try to find the spirit of this woman
and discover:
her love of apples,
her lust for holding gilly flowers
to her heart,
five children kneaded by her body,
her body ripped apart by torture.
Alaíde of ideas and of flying,
when I toss your death far away from me
it turns into a meteor of justice.[1]

—Alicia Partnoy

THE YEAR 2000 MARKED the twentieth anniversary of her disappearance at the hands of Guatemala's military rule. Alaíde Foppa, the founder of *Fem*, the first Latin American feminist magazine, was a poet, a human rights activist, a college professor, a literary and art critic, a translator, a mother. In December of 1980, at the age of sixty-six, Foppa traveled to Guatemala on a mission as messenger for a leading guerrilla movement fighting against the dictatorship. She was at that time mourning the death of her youngest son, Juan Pablo, killed by the military a few months earlier. Before taking the trip that would end in her kidnapping and, as we learned years later, her death in the course of a torture session, Foppa left an amazing legacy. The last broadcast of her *Foro de la Mujer*, the pioneering feminist radio program in Mexico, was an interview with three young Quiché women. One of the young survivors, Guadalupe, was in reality Rigoberta Menchú.[2] Foppa had requested the broadcast to be delayed until her return from her country, since the program testified on human rights abuses against the indigenous population by the government of Guatemala.

When I reread the interview to include the information in this essay, something extraordinary happened. It was an episode of what I call Magic Marxism, my tongue-in-cheek name for some amazing coincidences that strike my life and further our struggle for social justice.[3] I had discovered that in the actual interview, Alaíde Foppa introduced Guadalupe (Rigoberta), as a twenty-three-year-old woman. I suddenly realized that while Foppa in 1980 claimed that Guadalupe (Rigoberta) was twenty-three years old, that was precisely Menchú's age *two years later* in December of 1982 when she told her story to Elizabeth Burgos Debray. Although the voice in the interview was clearly Rigoberta's, I started to worry about the sources of my information. The voice was unmistakably hers, but who had told me that Alaíde's last interview was with Rigoberta? Could it have been Elena Poniatowska, or Carmen Lugo, her close friends? Maybe it was Julio Solórzano, her son?

As a scholar who specializes in testimonial texts, and a survivor of state terrorism, I must admit that the whole "Stoll affair," with its questioning of Rigoberta's sincerity had triggered my preoccupation with certain facts. I am referring here to the public and heated debate generated by David Stoll's allegations that Rigoberta Menchú had distorted facts or lied when recounting her life and the atrocities committed against her people in Guatemala.[4] However, and because I had not been concerned about the source before finding this inconsistency around dates, I made an effort to remember. My first conclusion was that the tip about Guadalupe being Rigoberta must have come from more than one source; it must have been vox populi, common knowledge.

In any case, I was worried and began researching Rigoberta's life in exile. I just needed some verification of her visit to Mexico in December of 1980. I reached for Menchú's *Crossing Borders*, a book whose reading I had postponed until I could get its Spanish edition. I happened to open it on page 104 where it said, "My sisters and I spent the Christmas of 1980 in Chiapas." (Big relief! Chiapas was close enough to Mexico City, home of Alaíde.) I kept reading: "After that we went to Mexico City for two weeks. There we met Alaíde Foppa, a great Guatemalan intellectual. . . . We were the last people she interviewed before she was kidnapped."[5]

Although a preoccupation with the truth seems to be the driving force behind this episode, my emphasis on the way Rigoberta's voice came across, almost by magic, as if Alaíde's spirit was helping me solve this problem, illustrates my point: *testimonio* is *not* about truth. Rather, the form serves as a tool for building a discourse of solidarity with victims of state terrorism.

We must focus on what testimonial texts *do* and how they do it to understand their empowering potential. This paradigmatic shift from the content of written and oral texts to the "semiotic plane," where, according to Robert Hodge and Gunther Kress, events occur "linking producers and receivers and signifiers and signified into a significant relationship," helps us deal with the dynamics around and within those texts.[6] It adds perspective to our analyses of the effects of Stoll's accusations on academia and helps us avoid the bitterness, guilty feelings, and questioning of our goals as educators who seek to build alliances with the oppressed.

Recently in the US, progressive college professors showed an alarming disorientation at the accusations of siding with an "inconsistent" Rigoberta Menchú, one who tiptoes around events and details that concern her personal life but who unequivocally tells the collective truth of the genocide victim, so people will be moved to stop the killings. Many teachers confided to me that they were considering dropping the text from their syllabi, fearing that their own credibility and objectivity would be challenged by students and colleagues. Others told me of the difficulties in finding support from other professors to cosponsor invitations to Menchú to their respective campuses. Stoll's observations managed to stall the process of building solidarity around Menchú's testimonio, because of what I perceive as an excessive preoccupation with either the truth or the literariness of the text.

I can never stress enough that the central feature of testimonio is neither its truth value nor its literariness (or lack thereof), but its ability to engender and regenerate a discourse of solidarity.[7] In a testimonio, the victim is not just a pretext for selling books, as in many stories often fabricated for mass consumption by journalists or politicians. Through the act of testifying, through the creation of the testimonio, the survivors of horrendous abuse are empowered. They are no longer tortured bodies to be pitied or patronized; they became the central force in a process that makes a difference in their own personal lives and also helps to further their political agendas.

Embracing Hodge and Kress's definition of discourse as "the site where social forms of organization engage with systems of signs in the production of texts," I also rely on concepts from their book *Social Semiotics*, to examine the ways solidarity is built through nonhierarchical, paratactic relationships between diverse participants in the discourse—such as writers, illustrators, editors, readers—which occur on the semiosic plane.[8] I propose then a radical shift in our examination of testimonial texts from the "mimetic plane" that "(implies) some versions of reality as possible referents" to the semiosic plane. This shift can be explained as follows. Rather than asking ourselves if the words of the victim represent in all truth the real world of destruction that she wants to describe (mimetic plane), I advocate for an emphasis on the ways the survivor and her story build a web of solidarity relationships (semiosic plane). The role of corroborating the truth value of the victim's account is already performed dutifully by the courts of law. In our universities, we too often end up serving a judiciary function, propelled by the perceived need to build an authoritative academic discourse relying on the unequivocable possession of the Truth.

The work of Elena Poniatowska, author of several groundbreaking testimonial texts, is a permanent exercise in the construction of the discourse of solidarity.[9] In the summer of 2001, while doing research on Alaíde Foppa, I sought Poniatowska's input on the dynamics between scholars, writers, and those whose stories we want to expose in our search for social justice. Here is a fragment of our conversation.

ALICIA: I have observed in your work and your life all the ways you generate a discourse of solidarity, discourse not as a text but as a weave, a *tejido* around the oppressed. In such a discourse, in order for solidarity to exist the writer must descend from her high horse and stand at a nonhierarchical level not only with those she interviews but with their texts and the reader. A weave of relationships around these texts make the readers part of this discourse, encourages them to participate and become agents for change, forging alliances with those who are at the margins.

Your goal to build a discourse of solidarity is obvious in your prologues and in the way you open doors for whoever wants to work for the victimized. A clear example is what you did at the book presentation for *Acteal de los mártires, infamia para no olvidar* by Martín Alvarez Fabela, when you addressed the audience and publicly thanked the author "for the honor of allowing [you] to write a preface."

However, when the Mothers of Plaza de Mayo invited Ernesto Sábato to write a preface to a poetry book by the disappeared and when Enrique Fernández Meijide asked him for a blurb for his collection on the disappearance of his son, Sábato avoided giving both the Mothers and Fernández Meijide any credit as writers or poets but just referred to them as people who suffer. Even publishers and intellectuals who, like Sábato, are allies, create these drawbridges that for some reason they lift when they are not clear about how to build this discourse of solidarity. Since you do not seem to ever "lift the bridge" from your side, my question is: How do you do it?

When you have Jesusa say "*ya no chingue*," you make her push the writer down off her high horse. This writer, this intellectual, goes to listen to Jesusa and she receives a lesson in humility: She is made to stand at the same level with the marginalized.[10] You seem to do these things naturally, with great ease. I don't know whether there are any recipes but since I come from the land of the know-how manuals, I seek some advice.

ELENA: I think everything is extremely intuitive and if there is a method, a technique, a way of doing . . . everything comes from journalism, because I started my work as a journalist, doing interviews. I've been interviewing since 1953. I never stopped. Yet with respect to the attitude . . . I can have an easy access to people like me, like my family, people with my same problems, aspirations, but I have always been interested, intrigued—I have developed a tremendous curiosity for the people I could not establish an immediate relationship with. For instance Martín, (Alvarez Fabela) moved me deeply. This young guy who comes from Toluca, with no money, suddenly he goes to Acteal and he becomes a witness to that massacre . . . and then he writes a book, very moving, very beautiful . . . and he is also committed to include photos, and he is so moved by what he has seen. . . . There was in him a true love for the indigenous people and I immediately talked to him and with what he said I wrote the preface. . . .

What I have always done is to approach people who even reject me for being *catrina* (snobbish) because my living conditions are not like theirs. But I have a tremendous advantage, Alicia, something I will never stop being thankful for: it helps me a lot being a shorty, *una chaparra*. My height helps me very much; it is a tremendous advantage for me because my physical appearance is not aggressive, I don't stand out. I'm as tall as those I interview and at times, they are much taller than me. Besides, I think they know that my interest in them is true. . . . And they also know that I'm in solidarity, that my interest is an "I'm on your side" interest and people know it, people feel it. That allowed me to go with the peasants, with the indigenous people, with the mothers of the disappeared.

In the course of the interview, Poniatowska gave me some extra advice. She told me to take advantage of the possibility of being in academia. She, the Teacher, my teacher, had been absorbed by journalism. It had sucked all her energy and it would have been "so good" for her to have a life in academia. Now, she said, she needs a triple amount of energy than before. However, even in academia, our energy can be sucked from us, and everything really meaningful can take us a triple amount of energy. On a day I felt somewhat depleted of that energy I played around the Internet looking for information about myself. Call it an ego boost or a little checking on the status of the discourse of solidarity, but I found a website,

Accuracy in Academia, that mentioned my name on a page entitled "The MLA's Preposterous Panels." The article read:

> Rather than the literary gathering it is intended to be, the MLA has continued their trend over the last several years in political proselytizing rather than serious discussion of the likes of Milton, Chaucer, and Shakespeare. The group's close allegiance with such organizations as The Marxist Literacy Group, Gay and Lesbian Caucus for the Modern Languages, and Feministas Unidas (Feminist United) [*sic*] has forced dispassionate and impartial scholarship to the back room while agenda-pushing has become the norm. After sorting through the MLA's over 800 panels, Accuracy in Academia presents the worst of the worst presented at the 1999 MLA convention.

And right there, in the sixth place of this list of the ten aberrations, appeared a panel "Writing from Prison," with a paper on Mumia Abu-Jamal's writings and another by Marie T. Farr (East Carolina University) titled "No Charges Were Brought Against Me: Alicia Partnoy's Tales of Disappearances and Oppression in Argentina."

Granted, Accuracy in Academia pushes the most conservative trends in our field to the point of caricature. However, both its righteous defense of "literary truths," and its fierce outrage in the face of our discourse of solidarity, give me a clue: Everything is wrong with building a discourse of solidarity in academia. We have to either dismantle or go against the grain of the discourse of academia. Both discourses cannot possibly coexist when we teach and center our lives as scholars on testimonial texts. We have to become shorties, *chaparritas*, and if we do it, we disappear. And I don't use the term lightly.

Since my own disappearance at the hands of the military dictatorship in Argentina, I have explored a myriad of ways to tell about those who did not survive and to demand justice on their cases.[11] In that quest, I have struggled to access as many spaces as possible with my testimony, and even when the notion of being a Writer, one of the few "gifted to publish," carries for me a weight of elitism, I have posed as one when necessary. I also pose as a Scholar to access other spaces. However, to pose as a scholar requires a tremendous amount of stamina. It demands that we be in conversation with scholars in papers, in journals, and not just in our heads. It forces us to transcend the "dissertation limbo" with whatever was concocted for the sake of our PhD degrees and to master academese. It forces us to be tall beyond comfort.

Just because I am so far from perfecting my number yet, John Beverley—who arguably has the most solid body of scholarship in the field of Latin American testimonial texts—does not know I've been in an ongoing, private conversation with him on the issue of solidarity and testimonio. I have always admired his ability to be short in terms of the discourse of solidarity around Rigoberta's testimony and tall in terms of the discourse of Academia. Part of his shape-shifting ability has to do with his obsession with that key feature of the discourse of academia mentioned above: Truth. Although Beverley had already pinpointed in 1989 that "testimonio has been important in maintaining and developing the practice of international human rights and solidarity movements," he still saw that "testimonio promises by definition to be primarily concerned with sincerity rather than literariness."[12]

When seeking to agree with George Yúdice's statement that the dichotomy of truth/fiction lacks any relevance to testimonio, Beverley arrived in 1990 at "a problem that I cannot solve. (It might be impossible to solve it conceptually because to solve it demands a cultural revolution.)"[13]

Tempting as it is, especially for people who, like me, risked their lives for a revolution, I believe there is no real need for such a drastic response. Rather than producing an entire cultural revolution, we could shift our focus to the ripple effect of revolutionary movements in Latin America, the ways the discourse of solidarity regenerates and involves us, university professors and our students in the US. If testimonio scholars had focused on this, we would have understood better, we would not have bled so much at Stoll's attacks, we would have prided ourselves for being targeted as participants in such a well-built discourse of solidarity.

If scholars interested in the voice of the witness had not privileged truth and literariness in their approach, professors would have included a wider variety of testimonial texts in their teaching curricula. Perhaps they would have taken its Cinderella, testimonial poetry, more frequently to the ball. Testimonial poetry. Nothing further from the truth of the witness as we know it in academia and the courts of law!

One of Beverley's many merits is his ability to revisit his assumptions on testimonio, the mediated narrative of the victim, and its paradigmatic text, *I, Rigoberta Menchú*. In doing so, he has shed much light on the issue. In *Subalternity and Representation*, he discusses solidarity relationships between scholars and testimonio producers, and he solves the problem that had haunted him nine years earlier. He does so by concentrating on the analysis of the semiosic plane and focusing on the relationships between text producers, readers, and scholars. I can't agree more with his assertion that "the subaltern . . . cannot be adequately represented by literature or in the university, that literature and the university are among the practices that create and sustain subalternity."[14]

However, some of us are not interested in representing the subaltern, but in empowering her, as well as in educating our students and steering them in directions outside academia and into action so the subaltern is no longer subalternized, deprived of human dignity, no longer massacred with impunity. Beverley has perhaps arrived at the same conclusion when he alludes to his wish that elite students feel "uncomfortable rather than virtuous when they read" these texts. He further elaborates, "What *I, Rigoberta Menchú* forces us to confront is not the subaltern as a represented victim of history, but rather as agent of a transformative historical project that aspires to become hegemonic in its own right."[15]

Paradoxically, to arrive at this bright conclusion, Beverley tackles Stoll's questioning of Menchú with the following challenge: "But the point remains: if the power of testimonio is ultimately grounded in the presumption of witnessing and speaking truth to power, then any evidence of 'invention' should be deeply troubling."[16] I find this assertion far too grounded in the discourse of academia, the politeness of academia, the text/scholar centered world of academia. I stand in shock at this realization, because I see Beverley as one of the most committed participants in the construction of the discourse of solidarity around Menchú, a participant with a very clear agenda in terms of validating testimonio and opening spaces so it can exercise its power in our classrooms. The way he tiptoes between the discourse of academia and the discourse of solidarity illustrates how, in its absolute privileging of Truth, academia fiercely resists solidarity.

Beverley wrestles with the same problem in a more recent article entitled "What Happens When the Subaltern Speaks," in which he makes the bright observation that "it would be yet another version of the 'native informant' to grant a narrator such as Rigoberta Menchú only the possibility of being a witness, but not the power to create his or her own narrative authority and negotiate its conditions of truth and representativity."[17] However, even when he advocates for respecting Menchú's agency, he centers his argument around issues of authority and truth, which makes the reader wonder if Stoll, the "taller" of the two scholars, the one always on his high horse, is not perhaps setting too many of the rules for this discussion. If not, why would Beverley refer to the "*near* genocidal violence of the Guatemalan army and ruling class"?[18] (Emphasis mine.) Maybe John Beverley was absolutely right, and we do need a cultural revolution, at least in the academic world, to really solve the problems that teaching and researching testimonial texts pose.

In *Subalternity and Representation*, Beverley had argued that "part of the appeal of *I, Rigoberta Menchú* that David Stoll objects to resides in the fact that it both symbolizes and enacts concretely a relation of active solidarity between ourselves—as members of the professional middle class and practitioners of the human sciences—and subaltern social subjects."[19] I would say that this is not "part" of the appeal but *all* of the appeal. What really infuriates Stoll and the accuracy squads in academia is our building of a discourse of solidarity around testimonial texts. Beverley proposes a dramatic challenge, a proverbial call to arms when he writes that "[l]ike liberation theology, subaltern studies entails . . . the possibility of building relationships of solidarity between ourselves and the people and social practices we posit as our objects of study."[20] However, I think that this enriching possibility should not be restricted to the fields of liberation theology and subaltern studies. If the subaltern, the marginalized, the victimized by state terrorism has become the object of study in academia, one way to avoid their objectification is by fostering of relationships of solidarity, through which the subaltern, the marginalized, the victimized can become truly empowered, since she and her testimonial texts become the central force in the construction of the discourse of solidarity.

Now that the Stoll controversy is becoming stale, we benefit by going back to the refreshing approach to classroom semiosis presented in several chapters of *Teaching and Testimony: Rigoberta Menchú and the North American Classroom*, a book published back in 1996.[21] In her essay "Passion and Politics: Teaching Rigoberta Menchú's Text as a Feminist," Stacy Schlau writes that she has learned through women's studies that "[c]hanging what we teach, means changing how we teach." Schlau's approach to teaching by providing "a model for collaboration rather than competition" and stressing that "the processes through which we communicate knowledge are as important as content" illustrates the practice of building a discourse of solidarity while teaching testimonial texts.[22]

Another contributor, Teresa Longo, writes in her chapter, "Rigoberta Menchú and Latin American Cultural History: A Professor's Journal," that "[i]n order for [the students] to start seeing Menchú as an intelligent, articulate spokeswoman whose cause includes promoting international solidarity with oppressed Guatemalans, they need to go one step further. This additional step requires a serious attempt at objective . . . textual analysis in response to the question 'How do Burgos and Menchú achieve solidarity with their readers?'"[23] When Longo speaks of textual analysis she clearly refers to the semiosic plane. In one of her journal entries she illustrates how a particular chapter in Burgos and Menchú's book "promoted a sense of transcultural solidarity with Menchú" by exploring the relationships between the characters in the text like Rigoberta's mother, other women, and the students.

When we teach testimonial texts, we come to the realization, like Longo, Schlau, Beverley, and so many others, that we are immersed in a discourse of solidarity that nurtures social justice. This type of commitment is at times heralded in academia. A recent encouraging event was the 1999 Presidential Forum of the Modern Languages Association (MLA) Annual Convention, convened by Edward Said. Participant Noam Chomsky noted that since 1968, the MLA has moved in a positive direction, citing "a heightened sensitivity to oppression and injustice, and an enriched respect for other cultures" and "a substantial growth of popular activism committed to human and civil rights, sometimes reflected in congressional legislation and court decisions and imposed with varying success on an often unwilling executive . . . [and] much reduced tolerance for state violence and terror."[24]

Elaine Scarry, another participant, addressed the subject of "Beauty and the Scholar's Duty to Justice." It seems easy to agree with her opening statement that "the central social responsibility of a teacher is to teach" but she then proceeded to clarify that Edward Said invited forum participants to address the issue of social responsibility and commitment "outside the universities." But Scarry talked about what teaching does when "spaces inside and outside the university continually place pressure on one another."[25] According to Scarry, among the impediments to freely exercise the "Duty to Justice" are "the recognition of the fragility of one's efforts," and "[e]mbarrassment and fear of public scorn," which she further describes as a process in which "[t]he mind moves in the direction of a certain fact or piece of information, and suddenly it boggles; it flees on the grounds that perceiving that fact would require that one then say sentences about it aloud, and it would be embarrassing to make a fuss."[26]

That ability to "make a fuss" is what author and veteran political activist Dorothy Healey calls the "quality of indignation." She highlights its importance and promotes its exercise "if speaking out and being outraged is indispensable to you in terms of your own coherence."[27] But how much of a fuss can we make without being kicked out forever from the discourse of academia which, of course, includes the payrolls of academia? And aren't we experts in making a fuss, which is simultaneously expected from us and used to displace us from the discourse of academia? And what happens, how "short" can scholars, readers, and students become, when the fuss is made by the text or the testimonial subject? This is the fuss that Doris Sommer has cleverly identified as the secrets and the highlighting of differences that testimonial subjects use to make us descend from our high horse.[28] It is the fuss that, according to

Jennifer Browdy, translates into "defenses erected" against those "parasites" who, far from empowering Rigoberta as a survivor, turn her into a sacrificial victim.[29] It is the fuss that Poniatowska's character makes when she tells the writer, "*ya no chingue*." It is Verónica de Negri's indignation. The Chilean activist and former prisoner of the Pinochet regime reacted against the manipulation of the testimonial subject by scholars, politicians, and "professional experts," who disregard the discourse of solidarity in favor of the discourse of academia, or that of mainstream politics. De Negri wrote this poem to honor her son Rodrigo Rojas.

DEFINITIONS
In tribute to Rodrigo, on the seventh anniversary
of being burned alive by 33 soldiers

I.
How can they know, they who
never had a son burned alive?
These men, these women, say they understand
and they define the crime:
THAT IS THE WORST THING
THAT CAN HAPPEN
TO A WOMAN.
Some, take up
what they call justice
and go and change it,
Negotiating with our lives.
Others, more powerful,
protect the criminals,
protect even their names,
in the name of that which
they define

as TRUTH
and RECONCILIATION.

II.
How can they know, they who
have never been tortured
after their children were dragged off?
These men, women, say they know,
that they understand.
And they define the crime:
THAT IS THE WORST THING
THAT CAN HAPPEN
TO A HUMAN BEING.
And taking on what we've gone through,
they travel through the world making analyses,
writing books, deciding
who merits
being a prisoner of conscience,
even classifying them
as being either violent or nonviolent.
They say they understand all this
while they use it to accumulate
wealth that allows them
to have a protected life.
These men, these women, say it's all
for us, for those who suffer.
Yet they use our lives
so they can be called professional experts,
consultants to governments,
communities, organizations.
They negotiate with our lives
to protect us, so they say.

They say they understand yet they never listen to us.
They are the same ones who exploit us
and make pornography of our pain.

III.
How can they know, these men, these women,
who have never been raped?
They are the same ones who like
to take up the flag
of defense.
And they define the crime:
THAT IS THE WORST THING
THAT CAN HAPPEN
TO A HUMAN BEING.
They are the same ones who say they understand
who seize onto our lives and bargain with them.
They are the same ones who catalog us:
we, women, men, who were raped
with rats, we are the creators
of a psychological fantasy
necessary to subsist from one day to the next.
How can these men, these women, understand?
Perhaps they sensed that animal
moving desperately
to free itself of the trap?
But these men, these women, are the same
ones who define our lives,
negotiate with them, assail them,
abuse them, creating words
that are politically correct.
They define what is normal or abnormal,
what is certain or not certain,

what is violent or nonviolent
what is true
what is torture or not torture
what is painful or not painful.
They seize onto our lives,
crush them
beyond recognition.
And when we demand justice they tell us:
"IT IS TIME TO BE KIND-HEARTED,
to reconcile ourselves so that the country
can reconstruct itself.
ENOUGH OF DEFINITIONS!"
It is time that society
understands that as long
as the criminals go unpunished
there is no justice,
the truth cannot be known,
and respect comes
from understanding the pain
of others in all its magnitudes,
DEFINITIONS
aren't worth
a damn.[30]

Today, mass massacres take place in Colombia, in a war fueled by millions of American dollars that totally disregards the lives of those the authorities claim to protect. Today, a US plane makes the mistake of dropping a bomb on a wedding in a country it went to save from the grasp of religious fundamentalists. Today, it is more important to protect the oil fields than the cemetery fields where the bodies of those assassinated by Saddam Hussein's regime bear witness to the crimes. Today, the Palestinian children killed by the terrorist government of Israel do not make it to the front pages of our morning papers. Today, while the powerful wage a messianic war against the ghosts of terrorism and produce thousands of "lesser" victims, "collateral damage" worldwide, I choose to make a fuss in the classroom. I treasure the moments we build a discourse of solidarity that challenges destruction, and I renew my promise to continue being scrumptiously "preposterous" . . . and shorter, and shorter.

NOTES

A version of this chapter was presented at the MLA 2000 convention panel on Social and Moral Responsibility, arranged by the MLA Committee on the Status of Women and the Profession. My gratitude to Rosemary Geisdorfer Feal, who convened that session, and to Shonda Buchanan for her help in editing this paper.

1. The epigraph is a poem entitled "Dialogue with Alaíde Foppa" published in Alicia Partnoy, *Volando Bajito/Little Low Flying* (Los Angeles: Red Hen Press, 2006), 57. The Spanish original is *"No se puede vivir/con una muerte dentro:/hay que elegir/entre arrojarla lejos/ como fruto podrido/o al contagio/dejarse morir."* —Alaíde Foppa. *"Busco el espíritu de esta mujer/y encuentro:/su amor por las manzanas,/ su ansiedad de alelíes sobre el pecho,/los cinco hijos que amasó/su cuerpo/ su cuerpo desgajado en la tortura./Alaíde de alas y de ideas/cuando arrojo lejos de mí tu muerte/se vuelve proyectil/por la justicia."*

2. A Spanish transcript of the interview and other valuable materials on Alaíde Foppa can be found on the website of *La Triple Jornada*, the feminist supplement of the Mexican newspaper *La Jornada*, http:// www.jornada.unam.mx/2000.

3. At the risk of killing the joke, I should explain that the label comes in handy to address the close-minded view shared by many US literary critics of all Latin American literature as oozing magical realism and, also, to mock the dogmatic view of revolutions in our continent as totally propelled by a Marxist ideology.

4. This debate was ignited by anthropologist David Stoll's allegations in his book *Rigoberta Menchú and the Story of All Poor Guatemalans* (Boulder, CO: Westview Press, 1998), regarding Menchú's statements

in *I, Rigoberta Menchú: An Indian Woman in Guatemala*, ed. Elisabeth Burgos-Debray (New York: Verso, 1984). A major academic controversy erupted around issues of truth and victims' accounts of events.

5. Rigoberta Menchú, *Crossing Borders*, trans. and ed. Ann Wright (New York: Verso, 1998).

6. Robert Hodge and Gunther Kress, *Social Semiotics* (Ithaca, NY: Cornell University Press, 1988).

7. Back in 1997, I wrote a dissertation that is still in dissertation limbo, a place called UMI Dissertation Services: "The Discourse of Solidarity in Testimonial 'Poemarios' from Argentina, Chile, and Uruguay" (*El discurso de la solidaridad en los poemarios testimoniales de Argentina, Chile y Uruguay*). (The text is in Spanish.) These concepts are further developed in that work.

8. Hodge and Kress, *Social Semiotics*.

9. *La noche de Tlatelolco, Hasta no verte Jesús mío*, and countless collaborations with photographers, prefaces, and works in anthologies like *El silencio que la voz de todas quiebra* about the hundreds of women assassinated in Ciudad Juarez.

10. "fuck off . . . ," *Here's to you, Jesusa*, trans. Deanna Heikkinen (New York: Farrar, Straus & Giroux, 2001), 303. I am referring to the character's reaction at the end of the book, once she has told her story to the interviewer. In the Spanish original work, *Hasta no verte Jesús mío* (México: Ediciones Era, 1993), 316.

11. The technique, practiced extensively by military dictatorships, consists of kidnapping a person, keeping her in captivity in a secret location to torture and eventually kill her. Bodies are not returned to the relatives. My experience as one of the few Argentine survivors is documented in my book *The Little School: Tales of Disappearance and Survival* (San Francisco: Cleis Press, 1986).

12. John Beverly, "The Margin at the Center: On Testimonio (Testimonial Narrative)," *Modern Fiction Studies* 33, no. 1 (1989): 19.

13. "un problema que no puedo resolver. (*Quizás sea imposible resolverlo 'en el pensamiento' porque requiere para su solución una revolución cultural).*" "*Introducción.*" *Testimonio, subalternidad y verdad narrativa.* John Beverley y Hugo Achúgar, editores. (Minneapolis: Prisma Institute, 1990), 15–16.

14. John Beverly, *Subalternity and Representation: Arguments in Cultural Theory* (Durham, NC: Duke University Press, 1999), 71.

15. Ibid., 82.

16. Ibid., 66.

17. John Beverly, "What Happens When the Subaltern Speaks: Rigoberta Menchú, Multiculturalism and the Presumption of Equal Worth," in *The Rigoberta Menchú Controversy*, ed. Arturo Arias (Minneapolis: University of Minnesota Press, 2001), 233.

18. Ibid., 224.

19. Beverly, *Subalternity and Representation*, 83.

20. Ibid., 38–39.

21. Allen Carey-Webb, ed. *Teaching and Testimony: Rigoberta Menchú and the North American Classroom* (Albany: State University of New York Press, 1996).

22. Ibid., 178–79.

23. Ibid., 306.

24. In *Profession* (2000), 33.

25. Ibid., 22.

26. Ibid., 27–28.

27. Dorothy Healey and Maurice Isserman, *Dorothy Healey Remembers: A Life in the American Communist Party* (New York: Oxford University Press, 1990). The quote is from Healey's speech "Women and Collective Memory: Ethics, Esthetics, and Politics" at an American University conference, Washington, DC, April 20, 1998.

28. Doris Sommer, *Proceed with Caution, When Engaged by Minority Writing in the Americas* (Cambridge, MA: Harvard University Press, 1999).

29. Jennifer Browdy, "Parasites and Polemics: Rigoberta Menchú and the Politics of Sacrifice," MLA 1999 conference paper; *Feministas Unidas* 19, no. 2 (Fall 1999): 31–32.

30. *DEFINICIONES. Tributo a Rodrigo, en el séptimo aniversario del día en que 33 militares lo quemaron vivo.* Published by permission of the author. Translated from Spanish by Richard Schaaf. In the original:

    I. *Definiciones (Tributo a Rodrigo en el séptimo aniversario del día en que 33 militares lo quemaron vivo).*

        ¿Qué pueden saber aquellos a quienes/nunca les quemaron vivo a un hijo?/Ellos, ellas, dicen que entienden/y definen el

crimen:/ESO ES LO PEOR/QUE LE PUEDE PASAR A UNA
MUJER./Otros, tomando en sus manos/lo que llaman justicia/
van y la transforman/transan con nuestras vidas./Otros, más
poderosos,/protegen a los criminales,/protegen hasta sus nombres,/
en el nombre de aquello/que definen/como la VERDAD/y
RECONCILIACION.

II.   *¿Qué pueden saber aquellos a quienes/nunca se les ha torturado/*
después de haberles arrancado/sus hijos?/Ellos, ellas, dicen que
saben,/que entienden./Y definen el crimen:/ESO ES LO PEOR/
QUE LE PUEDE PASAR A UN SER HUMANO./Y tomando
en sus manos aquello que vivimos/viajan por el mundo, hacen
análisis,/escriben libros y deciden/quiénes merecen/ser prisioneros
de conciencia,/hasta los definen:/violentos-no violentos./Eso que
ellos dicen que entienden,/lo usan para aumentar/los caudales
que les permiten/tener una vida protegida./Ellos, ellas, dicen que
es/para nosotros, los que sufrimos./Y sin embargo usan nuestras
vivencias/para hacerse llamar expertos,/ser consultados por
gobiernos,/communidades, grupos./Transan con nuestras vidas/
según ellos, para protegernos./Dicen que saben pero nunca nos
escuchan./Son los mismos que nos explotan/y hacen pornografía
de nuestro dolor.

III.   *¿Qué saben aquéllos, aquéllas/a quienes nunca se les ha violado?/*
Son los mismos a quienes les gusta/de tomar la bandera/de la
defensa/Definen el crimen: ESO ES LO PEOR/QUE LE PUEDE
PASAR/A UN SER HUMANO./Son los mismos que dicen saber/y
toman nuestra vida y la transan./Son los mismos que nos cat-
alogan:/quienes fuimos violadas o violados/con ratones, somos
creadores/de una fantasía psíquica/necesaria para subsistir./¿Qué
pueden saber ellos, ellas?/¿Acaso sintieron a ese animal/moverse
con desesperación para salir del atrape?/Pero son ellos, ellas mis-
mas,/ quienes definen nuestras vidas,/las transan, las asaltan,/las
vejan creando términos/políticamente correctos./Definen los que
es normal o anormal,/qué es cierto o no cierto,/qué es violencia or
no violencia/qué es verdad/qué es tortura or no tortura/qué es do-
lor o no dolor./Pescan nuestras vidas/las revientan/en una forma
difícil de reconstruir./Y nos dicen cuando pedimos justicia: "ES
HORA DE SER BONDADOSOS,/ de reconciliarnos para que el

país/se pueda reconstruir."/¡BASTA DE DEFINICIONES!/Es hora de que la sociedad/entienda que mientras/no se castigue a los criminales,/no haya justicia,/no se conozca la verdad/y exista el respeto/de entender el dolor/de los otros en todas sus magnitudes,/ de nada valen/las/DEFINICIONES.

15

DEATH IN THE DESERT

The Women of Ciudad Juárez

– Marjorie Agosín –

THROUGHOUT RECORDED TIME, poets, historians, and politicians have meditated upon the condition of exile and of the exiled—an experience that is exemplified in the mythical story of Ulysses, who in an attempt to defy the gods, remains outside of an Ithaca that he dreams and imagines and more than ever desires. For me, my exile had nothing to do with an expulsion or with the impossibility of remembrance, because somehow or other one always returns. Dictators perish and borders change. However, the desire endures. The desire for a fragrance or for the way in which certain vines cling to doorways. The desire to wake up and recognize oneself in one's own language but more than anything to be recognized by others.

In my years outside of Chile and Latin America, which add up to more than two decades, my desire has not ceased. On the contrary, it is a constant permanence or obsession that asks me for answers. My obsession turns its gaze toward the continent from the outside, to understand its passions, the depth of its pain and injustice.

My condition as an exile coincided with a fateful period in which cruelty, hatred, and impunity predominated. From the US, a country which had been responsible in large part for the Chilean military coup and its subsequent violations of human rights, my desire became a passion to reveal, examine, and understand what was happening in each region of the southern cone.

Poetry, which is always with me and brings me to privileged horizons and uncertain but always true pathways, beckoned me to look at, explore, and define that zone of political violence occupied by those who control history through fear. At the same time, however, I wanted to understand those who defy fear and create their own stories.

My commitment to the mothers of the Plaza de Mayo, to the women who make *arpilleras* and to the mothers of the disappeared arises from my condition as an exile who returns to the American continent with the capacity to tell, renounce, and be a witness of history.

I felt that through poetry and an intimate, pure, and authentic language, I would be able to sketch the grief and boldness of mothers searching for their lost children. This is how the collection of poems *Circles of Madness* arose—an homage that tries to honor and give relevance to the mothers of the Plaza de Mayo. Likewise arose an earlier book about the theme of political violence, *Zones of Pain*, which is written from the point of view of a blindfolded disappeared woman who tells, prays, and chronicles history.

Through my poems and passion to situate myself in the sectors of a dark and vanished history, I came to write the verses that form this present collection. I am referring to the poems about Ciudad Juárez, dedicated to the memory of the deaths of innocent women and to the cover-up and denial of the truth by the perpetrators. The dead young girls of Juárez, who were systematically raped, also have a profound relationship with the disappeared of Latin America—generations of idealistic young people who struggled for the possibility of a better world, out of an urgent desire for justice, peace, and the discovery of truth.

The poems continue to be recitations on grief, the politics of death, the application of justice, and the pronounced injustice suffered by the marginal peoples throughout a continent and a planet where women are victims of war, refugees, the raped, and the invisible.

My efforts also derive in part from a desire to reconcile the truth and the possibilities surrounding the truth. They are poems that came to me on a summer's eve as did the mothers of the Plaza de Mayo when I dreamed about the jacarandas or the night a painter told me how he dreamed of colors on the day they blindfolded his eyes.

The possibilities of language reside in the possibilities of faith; they are a form of redeeming and correcting world history and paying tribute to life in all its wonder. These poems were written by a spirit that wishes to be part of a history that does not cover but on the contrary reveals and is clear in the blinding light of every silence.

Y la noche era como un precipio,
Y la noche era un sonido ahuecado,
Más allá de todos los sonidos y todos los silencios.
Era la noche en Ciudad Juárez y las muertas de Juárez
Protegían a las vivas.
Y la noche no parecía ser una noche en la frontera.
Parecía mas que nada al sopor del infierno mudo
A las llamas que se transforman en cuchillos.

Y la noche en Juárez era un espejo perverso
Donde el suspiro de la muerte posaba sus cuencas
Y sus trofeos.

Y la noche en esa ciudad de Juárez no tenía ni principio ni fin
Tan solo el miedo
Tan solo la muerte.

— — — — — — — — — — — — —

And the night was a precipice,
A hollow sound,
Beyond all sounds and silences.
It was night in the city of Juárez and the dead women of Juárez
Protected the living.
It didn't seem like a typical night at the border.
It seemed more like the drowsiness of a mute inferno
And flames transforming into knives.

Night in Juárez was a perverse mirror
Where the breath of death settled its pits
And trophies.

And night in the city of Juárez didn't have a beginning or an end
Just fear
Just death.

Entre las nubes que apaciguan las tormentas
Yo las veo
Son las mujeres de Juárez
Girando entre las sombras.

Mientras los hombres de la guerra
Desfilaban con sus tanques y sus cuchillos
Yo quería comprender la posibilidad de
Seguir amando.

— — — — — — — — — — — —

Among the clouds that pacify the storms
I see them
The dead women of Juárez
Twirling among the shadows.

While men of war
Paraded with their tanks and knives
I wanted to understand the possibility
Of loving.

Con los corazones tristes
Como las amapolas cautivas
Otra vez ellas aguardan y aguardan
Llegan a la otra orilla
Algunas llegan
Algunas regresan.
Otras se encuentran como amapolas
Muertas en los desiertos
Algunas ya nadie recuerda
Algunas como amapolas rotas a las orillas
De todos los caminos.

— — — — — — — — — — — —

With sorrowful hearts
Like captive poppies
They wait again
They reach the other border
Some arrive
And some do not.
Others are found like poppies

Dead in the desert
No longer remembered
Like the wilted poppies
At the edge of the roadways.

Siempre al borde
Al borde de un camino
Al borde de la historia
Cortadas entre los bordes
Las mujeres de Ciudad
Juárez
Al borde de la muerte
A las orillas del miedo
Pueblan a una ciudad amordazada
Al borde de la sombra
Al borde del tiempo
Una voz sin cuerpo
Nadie.

— — — — — — — — — — — — —

Always at the edge
At the edge of the road
At the edge of history
Split between the borders
The young women of
Juárez
At the edge of death
At the shore of fear
Populate a gagged city
At the shadow's edge
At the edge of time

No body
Nobody.

Y de pronto la ciudad se convirtió en una sola luz, en una
sola mirada, en una sola historia. Las voces eran rugidos,
murmullos, como un terciopelo desgarrado, y eran voces
claras como los espejos del agua y eran voces que no dejaban
de preguntar y llamaban como en un susurro y llamaban en
el idioma del amor y llamaban en el idioma de la memoria.

– – – – – – – – – – – – – –

Suddenly the city was transformed into one light, one gaze,
one history. The voices were bellows and murmurs, like
torn velvet. They were clear, like water mirrors. They were
voices that didn't stop asking and called in hushed tones.
They called in the language of love, in the language of
memory.

En Ciudad Juárez las luces festivas
La música estridente
Las calles vestidas de rojo
Para ocultar la otra oscuridad
Del miedo
Del dolor clausurado
La oscuridad de los que mienten.

– – – – – – – – – – – – –

In Ciudad Juárez festive lights
Strident music
Streets dressed in red
To hide the other darkness
Of fear

Of cloistered pain
The darkness of those who lie.

Les contaré de ellas
Claro no son las señoritas glamorosas
Que viven en casa de cristal
La prensa ama recalcar la vida
De las desaparecidas con dinero
Con apellidos célebres
Con rostros de porcelana.

En cambio las desaparecidas de Juárez son pobres
Sus vidas son oscuras como su piel
Vienen de lugares extraños de la zona de Chihuahua
Algunos de Durango.
Son delgadas y jóvenes
Sin caras de porcelana.
Nadie conoce sus apellidos:
Hidalgo, Pérez, Fernández
Nadie desea conmemorar sus muertes
Las señoritas extraviadas de Juárez
No tienen dinero
Mejor no hablar de ellas.

Cada noche alguna muerte
Y en el amanecer es una prisión de miedo
En las ciudades fronterizas es posible
No llegar nunca a ninguna frontera.

— — — — — — — — — — — — — —

I will tell you about them
To be sure, they aren't glamorous girls

Who live in glass houses
Or fall in love with celebrities.
The press loves to highlight the lives
Of missing girls with money
With famous names
And porcelain faces.

But the disappeared girls of Juárez are poor
Their lives are dark like their skin
They come from strange places in the District of Chihuahua
Some from Durango
They are slender and young
And don't have porcelain faces.
No one knows their names:
Hidalgo, Pérez, Fernández
No one wants to commemorate their deaths
The missing girls of Juárez
Don't have money
It's better not to talk about them.

Each night someone dies
And daybreak is a prison of fear
In the cities along the border it's possible
To never make it to any border.

De María Josefina Hernández nada queda
Su madre cobija las prendas,
El vestido de percal perforado,
Los cabellos despavoridos.
De María Josefina tan sólo vestigios
Prendas distantes de lo que fue
Un vestido una blusa.

— — — — — — — — — — — — — —

Nothing remains of María Josefina Hernández
Her mother grasps the garments,
The dress of embroidered percale,
The terrified clumps of hair.
The only signs of María Josefina
Distant garments of who she was
A dress, a blouse.

De sus muertes tan
Sólo la muerte
Espectácular vacío
Ausencia ahuecada
Silencios pérfidos.
De sus muertes tan
Sólo interrogantes,
Rezos.

— — — — — — — — — — — — —

All we know about them
Is their death
Spectacular emptiness
Hollowed out absence
Perfidious silence
About their deaths
Only questions,
Prayers.

Los testigos son la memoria que
Recuerda a las mujeres de Juárez
Ahora estatuas,
Ahora huesos derramados,

Cabezas y orejitas.
Ahí se han quedado las mujeres de Juárez que
Han dejado sus alientos y sus vidas
Sus pasos sobre las arenas
Sus gemidos sobre mis manos que esculpen
Sus nombres en estas palabras
Que son rezo, plegaria.

— — — — — — — — — — — — — —

Memory is a witness that
Remembers the women of Juárez
Now statues,
Scattered bones,
Heads and little ears.

Remains of the women of Juárez
Who have left behind their breaths and lives
Their steps on the sand
Their moans on my hands that engrave
Their names in these words
That are a prayer, a supplication.

Noticieros

El noticiero de Ciudad Juárez
Anuncia otra muerte
Parece que es la misma mujer dice el niño
Todas las mujeres ésas son iguales, responde el padre
La madre desgrana alimentos
Se reconoce en esas mujeres
El noticiero sigue:

Anuncian los ganadores del torneo de fútbol
El niño pregunta a su mamá que por qué
Siempre matan a la misma mujer
La madre tiene una voz de extranjera
Una voz de niña
Y se hace un pozo de silencio
En su boca triste.

— — — — — — — — — — — — — — —

News Reports

The news report of Ciudad Juárez
Announces another death
The child says that it looks like the same woman
All of those women are the same, the father replies
The mother prepares the food
She sees herself in those women
The news report continues:
They announce the winners of the soccer tournament
The child asks his mother why
They always kill the same woman
The mother has a stranger's voice
A child's voice
And a well of silence
Forms on her sad mouth.

Larga y honda la noche
Del desierto
Todo y nada transcurre
Los pájaros meciéndose en el vacío
Del aire

El angel de la muerte
Los ahuyenta
Hoy como ayer
Otra mujer muere
En Ciudad Juárez.

— — — — — — — — — — — — — —

Long and deep is the
Desert night
Where everything and nothing happens
Birds rocking in the emptiness
Of the air
The Angel of Death
Chases them away
Today like yesterday
Another woman dies
In Ciudad Juárez.

Es posible que la justicia
Ante la muerte
Elegía a sus almas
Para la protección
Prefería a las muchachas rubias
Y blancas
Aquellas de los suburbios
Y de padres obedientes en el orden
De los deberes,
Padres de ocupaciones obsesivas
Amadores de todo tipo de posesiones
Inclinado a sólo palpar al mundo
A través de las imágenes.

Y la justicia
Protegía a la niña millonaria
Vestida de mujer
O a la religiosa de Iowa
O a las mujeres niñas que tenían
Historias de amor con políticos.

Siempre cautelosa la justicia con elecciones,
Aludiendo a las etnias, al color de la piel.

Y los habitantes de América
Miran con deleite extasiados
Algunos son muy hábiles en el arte de llorar.

En cambio
En aquella ciudad fronteriza,
Con olor a muerte a desagües
Putrefactos con voces de mejicanos
Pululando entre el sopor de un calor de bestias,
La justicia se olvida de las muertes de Juárez.
La policía bosteza
Unos dicen que andaban vestidas con ropas
Cortas demasiado cortas
Provocando a los asesinos que despúes
De todo eran hombres buenos.

La muerte llega a Juárez
Vestida de pobre
No usa tacos glamorosos
No mantones de manila.
Es terca

Sabe que nadie notará sus idas y venidas
Tan sólo las madres
Que creen que el alma regresa
Pero a Juárez nadie regresa.

La justicia sólo se ocupa de las niñas blancas
En las casas de vidrio.

— — — — — — — — — — — — —

It is possible that justice
Chose its souls
For protection
It preferred blonde girls
And white ones
Those from the suburbs
With obedient parents
In the order of duties
Parents with obsessive occupations
Fond of all types of possessions
Inclined to only touch the world
Through images.

And Justice
Protected the millionaire girl
Dressed as a woman
Or the nun from Iowa
Or the young women who had
Love affairs with politicians.

Always cautious with its choices,
Justice heeded ethnicities and skin color.

And the residents of America
Gaze enraptured with delight
Some are very skillful in the art of crying.

But
In that border town,
With smells of death and sewers
Putrid with the voices of Mexicans
Swarming amid the stupor of a bestial heat.

Justice forgets about the dead women of Juárez
The police yawn
Some say they walked around dressed in short clothes
Much too short
Provoking the murderers who
After all, were good men.

Death comes to Juárez
Dressed as a poor girl
It doesn't wear elegant clothing
Or embroidered shawls.
It is stubborn
And knows that no one will notice its comings and goings
Only the mothers
Who believe that the soul returns
But no one
Returns to Juárez.

Justice only concerns itself with the white girls
In glass houses.

Atrévete
A una plegaria

Para las mujeres muertas
En Ciudad Juárez
En las orillas de los ríos
En los estadios de Santiago de Chile
En aquella montaña cerca
Del Mazote, en El Salvador
Cuando se las llevaron a ellas
A las niñas diminutas con sus
Muñecas de trapo.

Una plegaria para las mujeres vendadas
Que se les negó el derecho al don y a la palabra
Una plegaria
Para no decir lo que no se dice
Para rezar como se debe
Para cuestionar al cuerpo de los
Sacerdotes uguentando al cuerpo
De las niñas
En el nombre de Dios.

Y en el nombre de Dios
Pongo en tela de juicio a sacerdotes
Y a los dueños de compañías
Porque las escondieron en los closets

Porque las obligaron a ser una sombra vigilada
En el nombre de Dios.

Una plegaria
Una estrella
Una flor
Para las mujeres de Juárez

Para todas nosotras
Para ellas.

— — — — — — — — — — — — — —

Dare
To offer a supplication
For the dead women
Of Ciudad Juárez
On the banks of the rivers
In the stadiums of Santiago de Chile
On that mountain near
El Mozote in El Salvador
Where they took them away
Young girls as petite as their
Rag dolls.

A prayer for the blindfolded women
Who were denied the right of free speech.
A supplication
To speak the unspoken,
To pray as one should
To question priests
Anointing the bodies
Of girls
In the name of God.

And in the name of God
I cast in doubt the priests
And heads of companies
Because they hid them in closets
And forced them to be supervised shadows
In the name of God.

A supplication
A star
A flower
For the women of Juárez
For all of us,
For them.

16

I CAME TO HELP

Resistance Writ Small

– Julia Alvarez –

RECENTLY, I PUBLISHED A historical novel about the poet Salomé Ureña, a poor mulatta girl, born in 1850, who became *la musa* of her young *patria*. It was Salomé who wrote the poems that inspired the young patriots who had just established the new free republic of Santo Domingo. In 1878, she became the first person to win the National Medal in Poetry in the Dominican Republic. This at a time when women were not taught to read and write so they could not respond to love letters.

But then, at the height of her fame, Salomé virtually gave up writing to start the first school for women in the country. She realized that it was *una indecencia* to be writing poems that only one half of the population could read, that her own gender couldn't access. She was going to build a nation, girl by girl!

Her daughter, Camila, was very different from her mother. She lived a placid, seemingly conservative life, teaching Spanish at Vassar for twenty years. But finally, in 1960, when she was sixty-four, she gave up her tenure and her pension to go to Cuba and be part of the literacy brigade there. When asked years later by her students and colleagues why she gave up her security and status at Vassar to come to Cuba at a time when so many were leaving the island, she said simply, without any fanfare, "*Vine a ayudar.*" I came to help. This comment by Camila gives me courage by reminding me that the way we really change things is often through very simple actions, small and quiet enough not to draw too much attention: a group of women wearing kerchiefs and black dresses and practical tie shoes circle a plaza in Argentina. A young woman in a threatened forest hugs a tree. Another and another join her. A handful of women in a Greek village refuse to sleep with their husbands until they end a war. A housewife in Southern France opens the back door and ushers her Jewish neighbors to the cellar of her house.

Vine a ayudar. I came to help.

I love the simplicity and sweetness of the statement, the respect for human life at its most humble level, the hand outstretched. Toni Morrison put it this way: "The function of freedom is to free someone else." This is the smallest atom of liberation that dictatorships and even revolutionaries often miss—dictatorships because they are looking out for the big counteroffensives and enemies; and revolutionaries because they often mistakenly copy the power structures of those they are struggling to resist.

I want to posit the small, sometimes invisible but utterly powerful way that we can be a force for change.

I trust that connective, consensus-building, hands-on process which I think of as a traditionally female process with its roots in the kitchen, women working together. Here, let me help you with that.

NO PARE, SIGUE SIGUE
Refilling the Resistance Well

– Veronica Chambers –

MY GRANDMOTHER, Flora Jean de Baptiste, born in Martinique, who came of age in Panama, ironed clothes for a living in the 1950s. She was a brown woman in a Caribbean country where Americans had instituted a paper-bag rule. If your skin tone was lighter than a paper bag, you were paid a gold wage. If you were darker, you were paid a silver wage. There were other separations too: segregation making its insipid way through our country: pitting cousin against cousin, sister against sister. She was poor. Her only daughter died in childbirth, leaving her eight grandchildren to raise in a one-room apartment. She taught me that every day your eyes open is a win. She said that every time you can put food on a plate and feed the people you love, you triumph. My abuela Flora told me that when you walk down the hall at five o'clock and you don't smell something cooking from your neighbor's apartment, you send a plate. You don't wait to be asked to give. She had so little and battled so much, but she was not powerless.

When my grandmother taught me to iron shirts, I was ten years old. She taught me how to test the heat of the iron without burning myself by throwing a few drops of water and waiting for the telltale sizzle. That year, I started ironing shirts to earn money for books. Twenty-five cents a shirt. The heavy iron in my hand. The coins offered in exchange for my work. We were poor, but I had something I'd never had before—spending money. I was not powerless.

My friend Carmen, Dominicana with a little *china* thrown in for good measure, hails from the same stock of women that I do, from the same stock of women that make up this anthology. We have been daughters and granddaughters, wives and sisters, *primas* and *prima-hermanas*. Now we are both mothers and it is our job to teach our daughters, in the year 2017 and beyond, that despite what feels like a devastating blow to our democracy, we all must keep going. As the expression and then the popular song urged us, *No pares, sigue sigue.*

But how do we do it? How do we "don't stop, keep going"? One way is by reading anthologies like this. In this day and age of binge-TV watching, when you can consume a season of *Luke Cage* or *House of Cards* in a weekend and then be done with it, it's easy to close a book like this and think: been there, read that. I urge you not to let the reading of this book be a one-time experience. Buy a copy for (or share a copy with) a woman you love. Donate a copy to your library or a mobile library like Uniproject .org that brings books into the community. Plan on re-reading an essay from this book the next time you find yourself falling down a social media hole. Pick up this book the next time you realize you've checked your e-mail three times in the last five minutes. We must refill the resistance well. We must take a step back from the twenty-four-hour news cycle to be reminded of how far we've come, how much wisdom and power we've accumulated as women, as immigrants and new Americans.

The groundbreaking musical *Hamilton*, by Lin-Manuel Miranda, ends with a swelling rendition of a song sung by George Washington. In the song, Washington posits that we have no control over who lives, who dies, who tells our story. *Women Writing Resistance* offers a powerful counter to the argument of the founding fathers. We may not have control over who lives or dies, but we do get to tell our stories. We write our resistance, page after page. And we hope that the force with which we move our pens across the page can be matched by those who value life, democracy, equality, and humanity off the page, out in the world. It is tiring and humbling work, like ironing shirt after shirt on a hot Caribbean day. But the effort has a palpable result: just like wrinkles fall out of a shirt, solutions fall out of resistance and hope rises like steam when you put your back into it.

Rereading this book felt like breaking bread with women I have known, women I admire, women I hope one day to meet. To call it kitchen table wisdom may seem like not saying enough. But I believe that we are still planning revolutions at those tables, so I say it with deference and respect. In her Nobel laureate speech, Toni Morrison spoke of how the very reach of language is one of our most powerful forms of resistance: "Language can never live up to life once and for all. Nor should it. Language can never 'pin down' slavery, genocide, war. Nor should it yearn for the arrogance to be able to do so. Its force, its felicity is in its reach toward the ineffable." I feel that in this book as we come to the last page: force, reach, and joyful felicity.

ACKNOWLEDGMENTS

THIS BOOK GREW OUT of several years of teaching two interrelated courses at Bard College at Simon's Rock: Women Writing Resistance in Latin America and Women Writing Resistance in the Caribbean. As I worked with my students through many powerful novels, short stories, poetry, and essays, I recognized and became fascinated by the profound thematic, political, and sociocultural connections that exist among women writers from these regions, despite its vast geographic span and linguistic and ethnic diversity.

I am grateful to my students in these classes, with whom I organized many conferences at Simon's Rock celebrating the power of women writers worldwide. I thank Marjorie Agosín, Julia Alvarez, Margaret Randall, Emma Sepúlveda, Alicia Partnoy, Raquel Partnoy, Betita Martinez, and Ruth Irupé Sanabria for giving so generously of their time and talents at these events, as well as for their personal support of this project. Every writer included in this collection has been inspiring and stimulating to me and my students, offering a model of courage, integrity, and generosity of spirit—shining a light, through their writing and lives, into dark and disorienting times.

I want to thank Provost Bernard Rogers and Academic Dean Patricia Sharpe of Bard College at Simon's Rock for their support of the first and second editions of this project, as well as my outstanding editor, Jill Petty, whose vision, enthusiasm, and commitment made both editions possible.

This book is dedicated to women writers of resistance everywhere. May our struggles for social justice not go unrecognized, and may our visions of peaceful, just futures for our communities and our world become reality.

—Jennifer Browdy

CONTRIBUTOR BIOGRAPHIES

MARJORIE AGOSÍN was raised in Chile, the daughter of Jewish parents. Heeding rumors of the coup that would install Augusto Pinochet, Agosín's family left the country for the United States, where Agosín earned a BA from the University of Georgia and an MA and a PhD from Indiana University. In both her scholarship and her creative work, she focuses on social justice, feminism, and remembrance. Agosín is the author of numerous works of poetry, fiction, and memoir, and is the Luella LaMer Slaner Professor in Latin American studies and Spanish at Wellesley College.

JULIA ALVAREZ is the author of many novels, including *How the Garcia Girls Lost Their Accent*, *In the Time of Butterflies*, *¡Yo!*, *In the Name of Salomé*, and *Saving the World*; collections of poems, including *Homecoming*, *The Other Side/El Otro Lado*, *The Woman I Kept to Myself*; and nonfiction books, including *Something to Declare* and *Once Upon a Quinceañera: Coming of Age in the USA*. Growing up as a migrant between the Dominican Republic and New York, Alvarez explores themes of identity and cultural intersectionality in her work. She is currently a writer in residence at Middlebury College.

GLORIA ANZALDÚA was a pathbreaking feminist, queer, and Chicana theorist, writing in poetry, creative nonfiction, and memoir.

Growing up as part of a Chicano farmworkers' family in the Rio Grande Valley of Texas, she was the first in her family to study beyond high school and earned both BA and MA degrees. Anzaldúa coedited *This Bridge Called My Back: Writings by Radical Women of Color*, one of the most cited books in feminist theory. Her groundbreaking autobiographical narrative, *Borderlands: The New Mestiza*, explores her identity as a working-class Chicana lesbian feminist and is a founding text of intersectional queer studies. She died in 2004 of complications from diabetes at the age of sixty-two.

RUTH BEHAR is the Victor Haim Perera Collegiate Professor of Anthropology at the University of Michigan. The recipient of a MacArthur fellowship, she is known for her interdisciplinary thinking about the search for home in our global era and for works that straddle ethnography, memoir, fiction, and poetry genres. Her books include *The Presence of the Past in a Spanish Village, Translated Woman: Crossing the Border with Esperanza's Story*, and *The Vulnerable Observer: Anthropology That Breaks Your Heart*. Behar frequently visits and writes about her native Cuba and is the author of *An Island Called Home: Returning to Jewish Cuba* and *Traveling Heavy: A Memoir in between Journeys*.

JENNIFER BROWDY is an associate professor of comparative literature, gender studies, and media studies at Bard College at Simon's Rock. Through her writing, teaching, and workshops, she advocates for social and environmental justice. Browdy's new memoir, *What I Forgot . . . And Why I Remembered: A Journey to Environmental Awareness and Activism Through Purposeful Memoir*, is accompanied by her writers' guide, *The Elemental Journey of Purposeful Memoir: A Writer's Companion*. Jennifer has written for *Yes! Magazine, Kosmos Journal*, and many academic journals and volumes; she edited the anthologies *African Women Writing Resistance: Contemporary Voices* and *Writing Fire: Celebrating the Power of Women's Words.*

VERONICA CHAMBERS is a prolific author, best known for her critically acclaimed memoir *Mama's Girl*, which has been course-adopted by hundreds of high schools and colleges throughout the United States. Born in Panama and raised in Brooklyn, Chambers often invokes her Afro-Latina heritage in her work. In addition to publishing several nonfiction books, including *The Joy of Doing Things Badly: A Girl's Guide to Love, Life, and Foolish Bravery*, Chambers is the editor of the 2017 anthology *The Meaning of Michelle*, about Michelle Obama. She has written more than a dozen books for children and worked extensively as a writer and senior editor for major media outlets, including the *New York Times*, *Newsweek*, and *Glamour*.

MICHELLE CLIFF grew up in Jamaica and the United States. Educated in New York City and at the Warburg Institute at the University of London, she completed a PhD on the Italian Renaissance. Before her death, in 2016, she published many works of memoir, poetry, and fiction exploring race, gender, and colonialism, including *Claiming an Identity They Taught Me to Despise*, *Abeng*, *No Telephone to Heaven*, and *Into the Interior*. The longtime partner of poet Adrienne Rich, Cliff was the Allan K. Smith Professor of English Language and Literature at Trinity College in Hartford, Connecticut.

JUDITH ORTIZ COFER was born in Hormigueros, Puerto Rico, and spent her childhood traveling back and forth between Puerto Rico and the United States. She has published fiction, creative nonfiction, and poetry, including *The Latin Deli: Telling the Lives of Barrio*

Women, which was nominated for a Pulitzer Prize; a memoir, *Silent Dancing: A Partial Remembrance of a Puerto Rican Childhood*; several children's books, including *An Island Like You* and *Call Me Maria*; and several volumes of poetry, including *Reaching for the Mainland* and *A Love Story Beginning in Spanish*. Cofer teaches at the University of Georgia as the Regents' and Franklin Professor of English and Creative Writing.

EDWIDGE DANTICAT spent her childhood in Haiti, joining her parents in the United States as a teenager. She graduated from Barnard College in 1990 with a BA in French literature and then earned an MFA degree from Brown University. Her master's thesis, a semiautobiographical account of the relationships between several generations of Haitian women, was published as her first book, *Breath, Eyes, Memory*. She went on to publish *Krik? Krak!*, a collection of short stories, which was a finalist for the National Book Award; the historical novels *The Farming of Bones* and *The Dew Breaker*; and a memoir, *Brother, I'm Dying*, which won the National Book Critics Circle Award. Danticat has received numerous honors, including a MacArthur fellowship.

JAMAICA KINCAID grew up in Antigua, migrating to the United States as a teenager and attending Franconia College in New Hampshire. She worked as a staff writer for the *New Yorker* magazine and published her first book, *At the Bottom of the River*, a collection of short stories, in 1983. Her novels include *Annie John*, *Lucy*, *The Autobiography of My Mother*, and *Mr. Potter*. Her book of essays, *A Small Place*, explored the effects of colonialism in the Caribbean, and her memoir, *My Brother*, chronicled her brother's battle with HIV-AIDS. Elected to the American Academy of Arts and Letters and to the American Academy of Arts and Sciences, Kincaid currently teaches at Claremont McKenna College.

RIGOBERTA MENCHÚ, a member of the K'iche ethnic group, was born in 1959 in a small town in the Guatemalan highlands. Her childhood and youth during the brutal civil war in Guatemala were chronicled in her 1987 testimonial *I, Rigoberta Menchú*, which has been translated into many languages and read around the world. Her human rights work earned her the Nobel Peace Prize in 1992; she was the first indigenous woman and among the youngest people to win that award. Menchú has become an international spokesperson for indigenous rights, serving as a United Nations Goodwill Ambassador and helping to draft and enact the Universal Declaration of the Rights of Indigenous Peoples, adopted by the UN in 2007.

CHERRÍE L. MORAGA is Chicana playwright, poet, and essayist. The coeditor of *This Bridge Called My Back: Writings by Radical Women of Color*, which won the Before Columbus American Book Award, she is also the author of the multigenre personal narrative *Loving in the War Years: Lo Que Nunca Pasó Por Sus Labios* and of two collections of essays on Chicano/a arts and culture, *The Last Generation* and *A Xicana Codex of Changing Consciousness—Writings 2000–2010*. Moraga has also published three volumes of drama: *Heroes and Saints and Other Plays*, *Watsonville/Circle in the Dirt*, and *The Hungry Woman*. She has served for more than twenty years as an artist in residence in the Department of Drama at Stanford University and also teaches in the Center for Comparative Studies in Race and Ethnicity at Stanford. She is a founding member of La Red Xicana Indígena, an advocacy network of Chicanas working in education, the arts, spiritual practice, and indigenous women's rights.

AURORA LEVINS MORALES was born in Indiera, Puerto Rico, to a Puerto Rican mother and Jewish father. Raised on the island and then in Chicago, Morales became an activist at an early age, joining the Puerto Rican Socialist Party, New Jewish Agenda, and radical cultural groups such as La Peña and the Berkeley Women's Center. A contributor to *This Bridge Called My Back*, she has also published a memoir, *Getting Home Alive*, and the essay collections *Remedios: Stories of Earth and Iron from the History of Puertorriqueñas*, *Medicine Stories: History, Culture and the Politics of Integrity*, and *Kindling: Writings On the Body*. Through her experience of living with chronic illness, she has alchemized what she calls "homeopathic activism" and aims to tell "stories with medicinal powers."

ALICIA PARTNOY, a poet, memoirist, scholar, and human rights activist, is a survivor of the secret detention camps where about thirty thousand Argentineans "disappeared." She wrote about this in her book *The Little School: Tales of Disappearance and Survival in Argentina*, which has been translated into several languages. *The Little School* was used as evidence in trials against genocide perpetrators who terrorized Argentina in the 1970s. Partnoy is the author of several other books, including the bilingual poetry collections *Little Low Flying/Volando bajito*, *Revenge of the Apple/Venganza de la manzana*, and *Flowering Fires/Fuegos florales*. An associate professor at Loyola Marymount University, Partnoy also presides over Proyecto VOS/Voices of Survivors, which brings survivors of state-sponsored violence to lecture at US universities.

RAQUEL PARTNOY is a painter, poet, and essayist. Born in Argentina, she moved to Washington, DC, in 1994 where she continued her artistic and literary careers. Her paintings have been shown in more than a hundred solo exhibits in Washington at Studio Gallery, the Embassy of Argentina, the B'nai B'rith Klutznick National Jewish Museum, Parish Gallery, and the DC Jewish Community Center, as well as at Goucher College in Baltimore and the Latino Art Museum in Pomona, California. Partnoy has lectured widely on women's art, the history of women of the tango, and her own experiences as a mother under a military regime.

MARGARET RANDALL is a feminist poet, writer, photographer, and social activist. Born in New York City in 1936, she moved to Mexico in the 1960s, where she cofounded and edited the bilingual literary journal *El Corno Emplumado/The Plumed Horn*. Later, working as an oral historian, journalist, and photographer, she lived in Cuba from 1969 to 1980 and then moved to Nicaragua for the first four years of the Sandinista project. In 1984, Randall came home to the United States but was deported when the government invoked the 1952 McCarran-Walter Immigration and Nationality Act, judging that the opinions expressed in some of her books were "against the good order and happiness of the United States." She appealed the ruling, winning her case in 1989. Randall is the author of more than a hundred books, including *Haydée Santamaría, Cuban Revolutionary: She Led by Transgression, Che on My Mind*, and *Only the Road/Solo El Camino: Eight Decades of Cuban Poetry*, as well as the oral histories *Cuban Women Now* and *Sandino's Daughters*. Since 1984, she has lived in Albuquerque with her life companion, the painter and teacher Barbara Byers; they were finally able to marry in 2013.

RUTH IRUPÉ SANABRIA was born in Argentina and raised in Washington, DC. She earned her MFA in poetry from New York University. She has read her poetry in libraries, prisons, schools, parks, bars, and universities across the United States, Mexico, and Peru, and her poems have appeared in anthologies such as *Poets Against the War* and *U.S. Latino Literature Today*. Her collections include *The Strange House Testifies* and *Beasts Behave in Foreign Lands*. She now works as a high school English teacher and lives with her husband and three children in Perth Amboy, New Jersey.

EMMA SEPÚLVEDA was born in Argentina and raised in Chile. She attended the University of Chile in Santiago until the coup d'etat of 1973. She immigrated to the United States in 1974; completed her BA and MA at the University of Nevada, Reno; and earned a PhD from the University of California, Davis. She is the author of more than twenty-five books, including works of poetry, fiction, nonfiction, photography, literary criticism, and textbooks. Sepúlveda worked for many years with the Chilean women's movement (Arpilleristas) and was awarded a Thornton Peace Prize for her human rights work. In 2004, she was named a Reno Foundation Professor in Foreign Language and Literature at the University of Nevada.

SELECTED BIBLIOGRAPHY

Abbassi, Jennifer, and Sheryl L. Lutjens, eds. *Rereading Women in Latin America and the Caribbean: The Political Economy of Gender*. New York: Rowman & Littlefield, 2002.

Alarcón, Norma, Ana Castillo, and Cherríe Moraga, eds. *The Sexuality of Latinas*. Berkeley, CA: Third Woman Press, 1993.

Alexander, M. Jacqui, and Chandra Talpade Mohanty, eds. *Feminist Genealogies, Colonial Legacies, Democratic Futures*. New York: Routledge, 1997.

Alexander, M. Jacqui, Lisa Albrecht, Sharon Day, and Mab Segrest, eds. *Sing, Whisper, Shout, Pray: Feminist Visions for a Just World*. Berkeley, CA: Edgework Books, 2003.

Arias, Arturo, ed. *The Rigoberta Menchú Controversy*. Minneapolis: University of Minnesota Press, 2001.

Bell, Beverly. *Walking on Fire: Haitian Women's Stories of Survival and Resistance*. Ithaca, NY: Cornell University Press, 2001.

Carey-Webb, Allen, and Stephen Benz, eds. *Teaching and Testimony: Rigoberta Menchú and the North American Classroom*. Albany: State University of New York Press, 1996.

Castillo, Ana. *Massacre of the Dreamers: Essays on Xicanisma*. New York: Plume, 1995.

Castillo, Debra, and María-Socorro Tabuenca Córdoba, eds. *Border Women: Writing from La Frontera*. Minneapolis: University of Minnesota Press, 2002.

Castro-Klarén, Sara, Sylvia Molloy, and Beatriz Sarlo, eds. *Women Writing in Latin America: An Anthology*. Boulder, CO: Westview Press, 1991.

Chancy, Myriam J. A. *Searching for Safe Spaces: Afro Caribbean Women Writers in Exile*. Philadelphia: Temple University Press, 1997.

———. *Framing Silence: Revolutionary Novels by Haitian Women.* New Brunswick, NJ: Rutgers University Press, 1997.

Edmondson, Belinda. *Making Men: Gender, Literary Authority and Women's Writing in Caribbean Narrative.* Durham, NC: Duke University Press, 1999.

Ghosh, Bishnupriya, and Brinda Bose, eds. *Interventions: Feminist Dialogues on Third World Women's Literature and Film.* New York: Garland Publishing, 1997.

Grewal, Inderpal, and Caren Kaplan, eds. *Scattered Hegemonies: Postmodernity and Transnational Feminist Practices.* Minneapolis: University of Minnesota Press, 1994.

Hoving, Isabel. *In Praise of New Travelers: Reading Caribbean Migrant Women Writers.* Palo Alto, CA: Stanford University Press, 2001.

Ikas, Karin Rosa. *Chicana Ways: Conversations with Ten Chicana Writers.* Reno: University of Nevada Press, 2002.

Kaminsky, Amy. *Reading the Body Politic: Feminist Criticism and Latin American Women Writers.* Minneapolis: University of Minnesota Press, 1992.

Kaplan, Caren, Norma Alarcón, and Minoo Moallem, eds. *Between Woman and Nation: Nationalisms, Transnational Feminisms, and the State.* Durham, NC: Duke University Press, 2003.

Latina Feminist Group. *Telling to Live: Latina Feminist Testimonios.* Durham: Duke University Press, 2001.

Lopez Vigil, María. *Cuba: Neither Heaven nor Hell.* Washington, DC: EPICA, 1999.

Martinez, Elizabeth. *De Colores Means All of Us: Latina Views for a Multi-Colored Century.* Cambridge, MA: South End Press, 1998.

Mohanty, Chandra Talpade. *Feminism Without Borders: Decolonizing Theory, Practicing Solidarity.* Durham, NC: Duke University Press, 2003.

Mohanty, Chandra Talpade, Ann Russo, and Lourdes Torres, eds. *Third World Women and the Politics of Feminism.* Bloomington: Indiana University Press, 1991.

Rodríguez, Ileana. *Women, Guerillas and Love: Understanding War in Central America.* Minneapolis: University of Minnesota Press, 1996.

———, ed. *The Latin American Subaltern Studies Reader.* Durham, NC: Duke University Press, 2001.

————, ed. *House/ Garden/ Nation: Space, Gender and Ethnicity in Post-colonial Latin American Literature by Women*. Durham, NC: Duke University Press, 1994.

Saldívar-Hull, Sonia. *Feminism on the Border: Chicana Gender Politics and Literature*. Berkeley: University of California Press, 2000.

Sandoval, Chela. *Methodology of the Oppressed*. Minneapolis: University of Minnesota Press, 2000.

Shohat, Ella, ed. *Talking Visions: Multicultural Feminism in a Transnational Age*. Cambridge, MA: MIT Press, 2001.

Smith, Bonnie G. *Global Feminisms Since 1945: Rewriting Histories*. New York: Routledge, 2000.

Springfield, Consuelo López, ed. *Daughters of Caliban: Caribbean Women in the Twentieth Century*. Bloomington: Indiana University Press, 1997.

Stephen, Lynn. *Women and Social Movements in Latin America: Power from Below*. Austin: University of Texas Press, 1997.

Williams, Claudette M. *Charcoal and Cinnamon: The Politics of Color in Spanish Caribbean Literature*. Gainesville: University Press of Florida, 2000.